Platform for Design

Hugh Pearman

Platform for Design

This edition published in the United Kingdom in 2016 by
Crossrail Limited: 25 Canada Square,
Canary Wharf, London, E14 5LQ.

Text © Crossrail Limited 2016
Design & Layout © Crossrail Limited 2016

ISBN 978-0-9933433-1-5

Writer: Hugh Pearman
Editor: Sarah Allen
Art Direction & Design: Andrew Briffett
Design: Chris Hanham
Contributions from Crossrail staff and its partners

Crossrail Limited is registered in England and Wales No. 4212657.
Registered Office: 25 Canada Square, Canary Wharf, London, E14 5LQ.

Platform
for Design

Hugh Pearman

Platform for Design

Foreword from
Andrew Wolstenholme OBE
Chief Executive Officer, Crossrail

By 2030 the capital's population is set to reach ten million and its transport system must be ready to meet this demand. The railway that Crossrail is building – to be known as the Elizabeth line from 2018 – is part of the UK's plan to maintain London's place as a world city.

The new railway will be a high frequency, high capacity service linking 40 stations over 100 kilometres, from Reading in the west to Shenfield and Abbey Wood in the east. It will reduce congestion by increasing central London's rail capacity by 10 per cent. It will create new routes into and through the city, giving 1.5 million additional people access to central London within 45 minutes. It will reduce journey times and deliver a world class accessible experience for the travelling public.

And what an experience! To deliver the new railway, Crossrail will build ten new stations, transform eight existing and upgrade another 22 to integrate with new tunnels and improved railway infrastructure to the east and west. More than this, the project is working with local Boroughs to improve public space around stations and with commercial developers to build new homes, offices and retail units above them. All this to better knit the new infrastructure into the communities it serves.

This massive contribution to the built environment of London and the South East has been planned with an intention to deliver a well-integrated new public service, designed to be safe, calm, spacious and accessible. Added to this is a programme of public art which is bringing some of the world's finest artists into our new stations to leave moments of joy and contemplation for the passengers of the future.

This book explains the design of public space for the Elizabeth line.

The Crossrail project is well on its way – and the railway is coming.

"The railway has been planned to deliver a well-integrated new public service, designed to be safe, calm, spacious and accessible."

"The new and upgraded stations and associated public space are the gateway to this new railway."

Foreword from Sir Terry Morgan CBE Chairman, Crossrail

Crossrail is much more than a construction project. It is an investment in London and the UK and a very real expression of confidence in the ability and skills of the construction industry as a whole. The Crossrail project will deliver a new railway for London and the South East. The Elizabeth line will increase capacity and choice and reduce journey times across the capital.

The new and upgraded stations and associated public space are the gateway to this new railway. To build these new structures - underground, below historic buildings, in constrained sites and amongst diverse communities – has been a major design and construction challenge. We have had to innovate, to harness the latest technology, prototype new materials and components and push established techniques to get the job done. The design effort has been considerable. Its success will be measured in the ease and comfort of passengers' use as they pass through the system from 2018 and beyond.

The most important thing Crossrail has done lies in its wider impact on the industry, particularly in its contribution to improving health and safety and innovation and in developing skills. Creating our Tunnelling & Underground Construction Academy, training the workforce and driving up the number of young people in the industry through the recruitment of over 500 apprentices have been some of our proudest achievements.

As the construction of our new stations and public spaces comes closer to completion, our activity moves to the fit out and installation of systems that will turn these stunning new spaces into an operational railway. This book recognises the contribution of every individual involved in the design and build of this new asset for London – and looks forward to the time when we will be able to show these new spaces to its future passengers.

The Elizabeth line

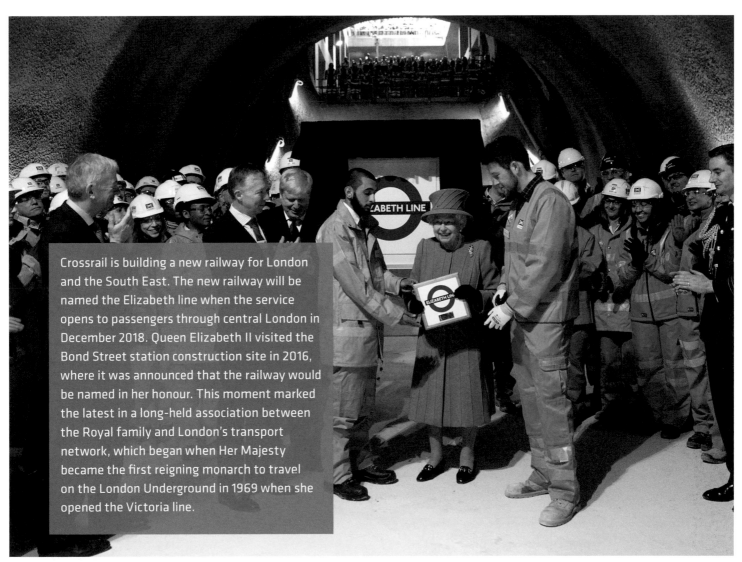

Crossrail is building a new railway for London and the South East. The new railway will be named the Elizabeth line when the service opens to passengers through central London in December 2018. Queen Elizabeth II visited the Bond Street station construction site in 2016, where it was announced that the railway would be named in her honour. This moment marked the latest in a long-held association between the Royal family and London's transport network, which began when Her Majesty became the first reigning monarch to travel on the London Underground in 1969 when she opened the Victoria line.

Her Majesty Queen Elizabeth II at Crossrail's Bond Street station work site on 23 February 2016

The history

The idea of an east-west railway under the capital has existed as a concept in modern times since just after the London Blitz, when – with reconstruction in mind – plans started to be hatched for a variety of mainline underground metro railways across London. Not that such schemes were anything new even then: Brunel wanted to link his Great Western railway across the capital to other routes. The original Metropolitan line from Paddington to Farringdon in 1863, running steam trains at first, was the equivalent of its day, while the Regent's Canal Company proposed another cross-London rail route approved in the 1880s but never built.

The idea appeared in a succession of reconstruction plans for London from 1943 to 1949 including the famous Greater London "Abercrombie" Plan of 1944. Decades passed, and these all eventually boiled down to the official intention to have mainline trains crossing London, both north-south (that at first became Thameslink, using existing lines, later massively upgraded and extended) and east-west. Hence Crossrail, which acquired that name for the first time in 1974 as a proposed system of two separate east-west lines that curved towards each other and touched in the middle.

By this time Paris was building its RER express underground lines, German cities had their S-Bahn equivalents, but London wasn't yet ready. More studies, with increasing detail, followed: by 1990 the line's route was safeguarded, and by 1993 architects were designing individual stations. At last it was possible to see what such a metro line beneath London and out into the surrounding region might actually look like. It looked very little like the Tube stations Londoners were used to. Everything about the proposed system was bigger, starting with the tunnels and the trains intended to run through them. These were to be much longer than tube trains, each carrying around twice as many passengers. To handle all these people – and to allow for population growth – the concourses had to be very large, while the length of the trains meant that most stations would need exits and entrances at both ends, complete with ticket halls and new buildings above them. A way was found to drop all this into a city already riddled with tunnels of all kinds, connecting to existing underground and surface lines at key points.

Added to that, the "New Austrian Tunnelling Method", first invented in the 1960s, was to be used for most of the stations. Using sprayed concrete rather than conventional iron or concrete curved sections meant that the shapes of the spaces could be much more adaptable as well as simply bigger. This led to some thoroughly romantic designs, with architects suggesting domed or egg-shaped concourses decorated like stage sets with everything from tropical forests and soaring angels to ornate candelabras. The decision was taken that the underground realm in central London should be by one set of architects and designers, while the individual station ticket halls and upper concourses, plus the buildings over them, should be by a roster of others. Some of the architects first signed up back then have delivered today's revised version.

Then another recession-induced delay set in and the 1993 version of Crossrail, all ready for construction to start, was halted. It was not until 2008 that an east-west Crossrail was finally enacted by Parliament. Its route is less complex than earlier proposals, though with a spur to Heathrow Airport to the West and another to Woolwich and Abbey Wood in the South East. Originally intended to run to Maidenhead in the west, the route was later extended a dozen miles further to Reading. In the east it terminates and connects to the Great Eastern Main Line at Shenfield in Essex. There are 40 stations in all. Of course the main passenger traffic will be through the central section of the route, relieving congestion on other lines through the city (plus a lot of Heathrow Airport journeys). But were you so minded, by 2019 it will be possible to take one train from Essex in the east through central London to Reading in the west (or vice versa). That will be a journey of just over 100 kilometres or 70 miles, taking 102 minutes. This distance redefines the edges of the capital's commuter belt.

A selection of early drawings from 1990's by BDP in collaboration with Ralph Erskine

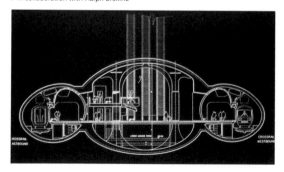

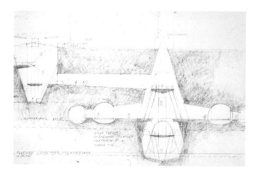

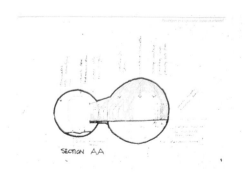

Today's context

It was fortunate that the project finally went ahead when it did, because London – which had been gently depopulating throughout the post-war years – had started to grow again from the mid 1980s, and the growth has accelerated since then. By early 2015 London's population stood at 8.6 million – close to its previous peak in 1939 when congestion had been a serious issue. By 2030 it is forecast to be ten million. The new railway could not come soon enough.

The design work from 1993 was revisited and refined. The key principles remained – especially the need to think big, to design and build for growth. The station locations remained fairly constant, but they were radically redesigned with larger, often multiple entrances and ticket halls, working in parallel with big upgrades to the connecting Tube and railway stations.

An important new criterion – sustainability, both in construction and in use – came into play, along with the need for full accessibility. Then came new thinking on low-energy lighting, better acoustics and air handling, and the overall finishes to the underground concourses. There, the emphasis switched to lightness, minimalism, clear orientation for passengers and tough, durable materials. Meanwhile the technology of everything from design co-ordination through efficient train design with onboard signalling to intelligent route information has progressed enormously. Today's railway is considerably more advanced than the one they almost built.

Construction ceremoniously began at Canary Wharf on 15 May, 2009. Despite the dire economic situation at the time, the main political parties all supported it: like the 2012 Olympics in London, it was seen as the kind of expenditure that could provide a Keynesian stimulus to the economy. This was indeed the case. It has been estimated that the railway could accelerate or unlock the development of 57,000 new homes and 3.5 million square feet of shops and offices along the route, whilst some 55,000 jobs are supported by the building of the line, yielding £42 billion for the UK economy. The effect is felt nationwide, since 95 per cent of the contracts went to UK-based companies including the manufacture of tunnel and platform components and the Derby-built trains. And 65 per cent of the appointed contractors come from outside London.

All the tunnelling across central London – in all there are 42 kilometres of new tunnels, ten all-new stations and many more upgraded – finally provide the necessary frequent, high-capacity rail link into which feed upgraded existing lines and stations from the East into Liverpool Street, and from the West into Paddington. At a stroke this provides the capital with 10 per cent more rail capacity, which translates into 200 million passenger journeys a year. It means that more journeys will be made by rail rather than road, so helping to tackle pollution. And by greatly reducing the need for passengers to interchange at the edges of central London, it relieves congestion at existing stations and on other lines. This will particularly improve on the existing arrangements for getting to and from Heathrow Airport.

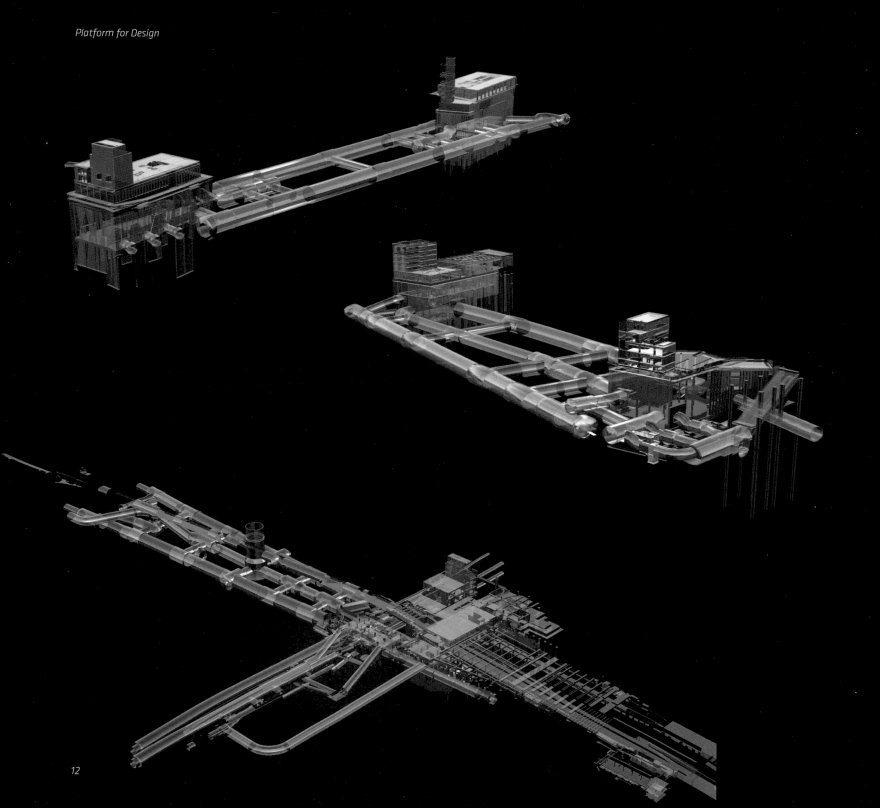

The roster of engineers, architects and designers has been working in a co-ordinated way, using a common virtual model of the entire system created in Building Information Modelling (BIM). In effect, the whole railway system has been built twice: once virtually, then physically. This method provides a common, shared source of all information. Built into this planning is a very high degree of sustainability, both in construction and in use: from the way excavated material has formed a new wetland nature reserve, to the advanced lightweight trains, designed to use power efficiently.

The usefulness of all this lies not only in the building of the Crossrail project, but carries on thereafter. The Elizabeth line, as it will be known, will need to be maintained. The virtual model knows exactly where every single component is, while built-in sensors for shorter-life electrical equipment, from LED lighting to massive ventilation fans, will monitor performance and spot impending failures so parts can be replaced before they go wrong in use, with easy access designed in. The trains are similarly self-diagnosing, for ongoing maintenance in their depots. The aim is to provide a very reliable railway indeed.

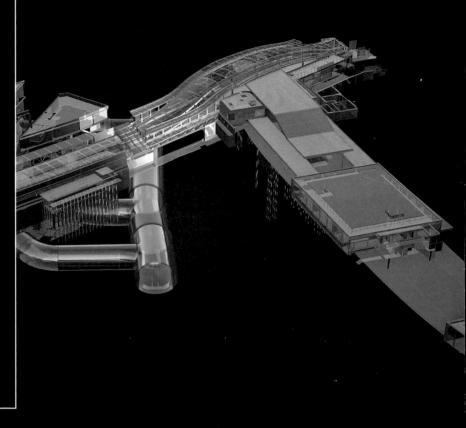

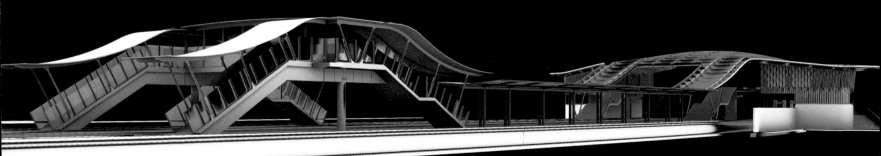

While most of that is invisible to the travelling public, other aspects of the project are highly visible, such as the commissioned public art programme that will distinguish several stations through the centre of London.

And it is not about stations in isolation. As well as the new stations and refurbishments, design thinking has extended beyond the station boundaries to streetscape improvements – sometimes, thanks to local authority, Transport for London and private partners - extending a considerable distance. 40 public spaces have been redesigned to improve access, crossings, cycle parking, greenery, totalling 190,000 square metres. There are commercial developments too. Healing some of the scars created by large scale construction are 12 new buildings - 3 million square feet of residential and retail space. These help embed the new railway into its landscape – and pay a considerable contribution to the cost of the project too. Designing all of this from pavement to platform in an integrated way is unusual and ambitious. The experience of passing through these spaces should be enhanced as a result.

Individual firms of architects designed the stations to have unique character, drawing on their local surroundings – often different at each end of these very long stations. Meanwhile down at platform level, consistency reigns: a team of other architects and designers has designed the common parts of the railway, working to detail the spaces established at the outset with the engineers: the broad, high concourse passages, for instance, are designed with gentle, flared corners so that nobody ever has to make a sharp right-angled turn, improving

visibility and safety. Wayfinding is designed with local information at platform level so you know easily which end of the station to head for. Visual clutter is minimised.

The project is also about urban regeneration on a wider basis than its above-station redevelopments. In a classical economic response, its existence is already stimulating a great deal of new building indirectly, because of the well-connected locations it creates. Its full effects cannot be instant – such is the nature of building and economics – but the capital will benefit by far more than the remarkable 10% increase in rail capacity that the railway provides. This needs to continue: hence the plans for further railways such as Crossrail 2 from South West to North East through the centre of London, and High Speed 2 and 3.

Until now, much of the story of Crossrail has been about its engineering marvels, in particular the work of its eight tunnelling machines, plus the individually fascinating stories of archaeological finds in the station excavations which help to reveal the history of London. Now – two years from opening at the time of writing – the aim of this book is to describe what the resulting Elizabeth line stations and public spaces will really be like, how we will experience the way its architecture and design defines its extraordinary spaces.

*Commercial development, urban realm and
station entrance at Paddington Canal-side*

← Way out   Dean Street

Emergency
stairs only

Design approach

The fundamental design of the Crossrail project reflects an approach adopted by a cohort of architects, engineers, designers and railway operators anticipating future passenger demands, as well as the constraints of building across the city and integrating with upgraded infrastructure in the suburbs.

Key decisions determined the basic structures of new stations– box or mined stations below ground and above ground structures. These decisions, influenced by location, urban density, heritage properties, integration opportunities, form the spine of each new station building.

Ticket hall at Dean Street,
Tottenham Court Road station

Underground mined stations are excavated by tunnelling, using tunnel boring machines and manual methods to carve out underground spaces and secure them with sprayed concrete linings. The method was well suited to congested and historic locations, where protection of heritage buildings above was paramount. Engineering technology for sprayed concrete lining of manually excavated spaces, extended for application on bigger spaces, helped deliver far larger mined stations than ever built before.

 Station Transformations Station transformations are designed to significantly upgrade existing facilities, providing new entrances and large, bright ticket halls, longer platforms and improved forecourts.

 Underground 'box' stations are created by concrete diaphragm retaining walls built prior to large scale excavation taking place to create a large box shaped void. The final structure is installed either from the top down or bottom up. The stations are characterised by huge, rectangular volumes, wide platforms and open designs.

 Above ground stations are designed to best suit local contexts outside of central London, to integrate with existing infrastructure and other rail services.

 Refurbishments are being delivered to improve comfort and accessibility through lift installations, platform extensions and ticket hall upgrades.

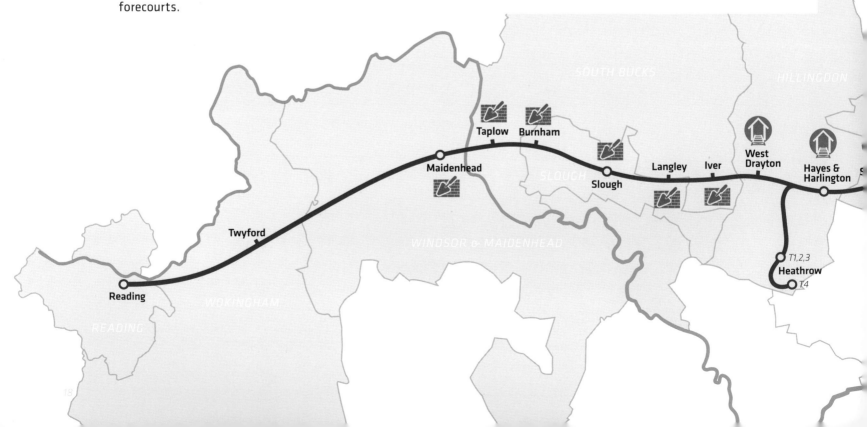

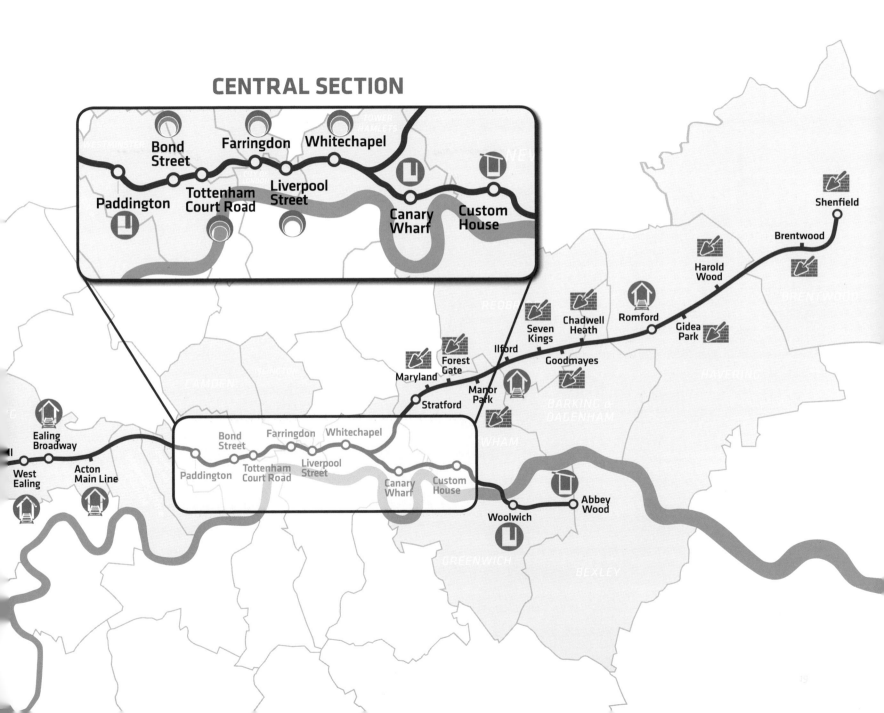

CENTRAL SECTION

Bond Street

Farringdon

Whitechapel

Paddington

Tottenham Court Road

Liverpool Street

Canary Wharf

Custom House

Shenfield

Brentwood

Harold Wood

Romford

Gidea Park

Seven Kings

Chadwell Heath

Ilford

Goodmayes

Forest Gate

Maryland

Manor Park

Stratford

Ealing Broadway

West Ealing

Acton Main Line

Bond Street

Farringdon

Whitechapel

Paddington

Tottenham Court Road

Liverpool Street

Canary Wharf

Custom House

Woolwich

Abbey Wood

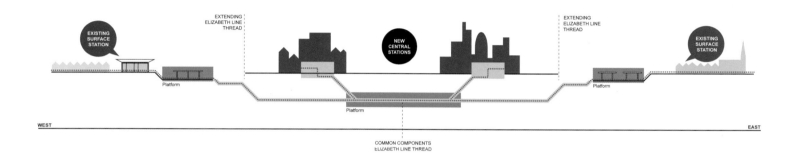

Seven key principles inform all design; identity, clarity, consistency, inclusivity, sustainability, security and a focus on people. Yet the application of the project's design language differs both along the route and from street to platform.

Features aligned to these principles include lifts and ramps at all stations to make the service accessible, honest expression of structural forms such as the sprayed concrete lined tunnels simply clad in new tunnelled stations, prioritisation of natural light and intelligent lighting systems, neutral colour palettes and smart design of services to aid maintenance for its 120 year lifetime.

The railway's design style is most intensely expressed in the centre of the route, on its new, dedicated infrastructure and particularly in the tunnelled spaces themselves. Here, consistent key principles, palette and components are applied.

Above, the new ticket halls will provide a response to their local contexts integrating into the existing urban fabric, while integrating a range of common components.

On the surface, where existing infrastructure has been upgraded a common palette and consistent products provide a level of the Elizabeth line identity.

A comfortable journey

Fundamental to the comfort of the Elizabeth line passenger but hidden from view are a set of thoughtful design decisions around the management of air and heat. In any underground railway, trains push air into stations as they approach and pull air out as they leave. They also create heat as they accelerate and decelerate. The larger the trains, the greater the force of air and heat generated. Add to this the ejected air from a modern train's air conditioning system and you could create significant discomfort for passengers on platforms – and store up long term problems for infrastructure – if it is not managed effectively.

The Elizabeth line trains will be 200 metres long, over one and a half times longer than any already used on the Underground and air-conditioned for maximum comfort. To manage heat and air a number of fundamental design decisions were made which will quietly underpin the design of its underground stations.

Screens will edge the platforms of the underground stations, first seen in London with the Jubilee line extension in 1999, but here extended to full height. While housing customer information systems to improve wayfinding and separating passengers from the tracks, one key job of the screens is to manage the flush of hot air generated by incoming trains away from passengers. Large voids have been designed under platforms and massive ventilation fans installed at every station. The hot air will be powered by these fans through the voids and out of ventilation shafts at the ends of the

stations. Hot air in the tunnels will be channelled out of the further shafts along the route. With these screens in place, air from above isn't pulled into the platforms by the vacuum created by departing trains, so a system has been designed to allow a constant circulation of fresh air during operational hours, which can be boosted to remove smoke in the event of a fire. While the passenger may never notice the deep platform edge housing the vents, they'll know the new stations are cool year round.

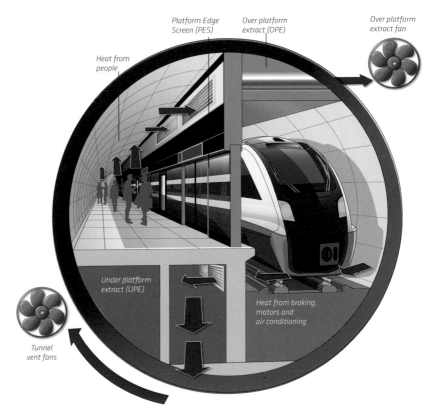

Platform Edge Screen (PES)

Over platform extract (OPE)

Over platform extract fan

Heat from people

Under platform extract (UPE)

Heat from braking, motors and air conditioning

Tunnel vent fans

Sustainable choices

Choices in the design of the Elizabeth line will make the railway a far more sustainable service.

Energy requirements have been reduced through prioritising natural light in stations, designing the vertical track profile to aid acceleration and deceleration, developing LED lighting for station and tunnel environments and specifying lightweight, energy efficient rolling stock and responsive escalators and lifts. Commercial developments above stations will benefit from technology to extract ground heat, built into the fabric of the stations below.

Environmental impacts have been minimised by reusing 98% of tunnel spoil to build nature reserves, restore land for recreational and agricultural use and by designing green features into stations and ventilation shaft structures. Sedum roofs will protect biodiversity and improve energy efficiency and solar photovoltaic panels will reduce energy requirements.

Having incorporated these and other measures, the Elizabeth line's new stations will achieve Very Good on the established building industry environmental rating scale BREEAM (Building Research Establishment Environmental Assessment Methodology).

Use of refurbished historic structures such as Connaught Tunnel, East London as part of the route and incorporating the frontage of the existing Whitechapel station helps to reuse resources more efficiently and preserve local character.

From social and economic perspectives, the building of the railway has supported 55,000 jobs, over 500 apprentices and awarded 95% of its contracts to business across the UK making a considerable contribution to the economy. When the railway is complete it will transport 200 million passengers a year and is estimated to deliver £42 billion in benefit.

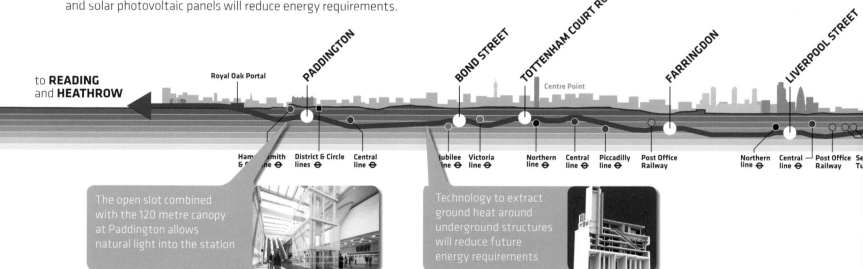

to **READING** and **HEATHROW**

Royal Oak Portal · PADDINGTON · BOND STREET · TOTTENHAM COURT ROAD · Centre Point · FARRINGDON · LIVERPOOL STREET

Hammersmith & City line ⊖ · District & Circle lines ⊖ · Central line ⊖ · Jubilee line ⊖ · Victoria line ⊖ · Northern line ⊖ · Central line ⊖ · Piccadilly line ⊖ · Post Office Railway · Northern line ⊖ · Central line ⊖ · Post Office Railway · Se Tu

The open slot combined with the 120 metre canopy at Paddington allows natural light into the station

Technology to extract ground heat around underground structures will reduce future energy requirements

Escalators are responsive to passenger flows, to reduce power usage

Terrazzo, made from waste stone, provides a sustainable floor surface for many stations

Lightweight lifts that use the energy they create when braking will reduce energy required by 20%

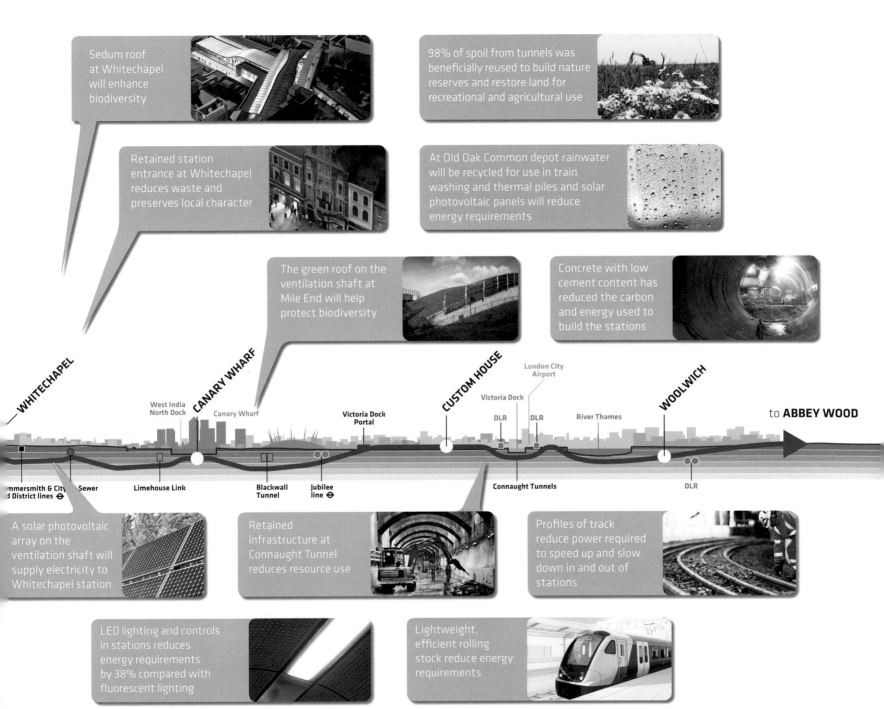

Sedum roof at Whitechapel will enhance biodiversity

98% of spoil from tunnels was beneficially reused to build nature reserves and restore land for recreational and agricultural use

Retained station entrance at Whitechapel reduces waste and preserves local character

At Old Oak Common depot rainwater will be recycled for use in train washing and thermal piles and solar photovoltaic panels will reduce energy requirements

The green roof on the ventilation shaft at Mile End will help protect biodiversity

Concrete with low cement content has reduced the carbon and energy used to build the stations

WHITECHAPEL
CANARY WHARF
CUSTOM HOUSE
London City Airport
Victoria Dock
WOOLWICH

West India North Dock
Canary Wharf
Victoria Dock Portal
DLR
DLR
River Thames

to **ABBEY WOOD**

Hammersmith & City and District lines
Sewer
Limehouse Link
Blackwall Tunnel
Jubilee line
Connaught Tunnels
DLR

A solar photovoltaic array on the ventilation shaft will supply electricity to Whitechapel station

Retained infrastructure at Connaught Tunnel reduces resource use

Profiles of track reduce power required to speed up and slow down in and out of stations

LED lighting and controls in stations reduces energy requirements by 38% compared with fluorescent lighting

Lightweight, efficient rolling stock reduce energy requirements

The well-tempered environment

As the Crossrail project turned from concept to reality, so did a secret underground station that existed on its own, unconnected to any of the others. Concealed on the edge of a Bedfordshire town some 40 miles north of London, it had two platforms and a connecting passageway for passengers, a live overhead wire for the (mysteriously absent) trains, an escalator, a variety of signs, seats, lighting, balustrades, PA systems, pretty much everything you'd expect to find down at platform level when the Elizabeth line opens in 2018.

But not all these parts were arranged in order. They all seemed real, but while some were solid, others sounded strangely hollow when you tapped them. In one place the signs told you

FACTS & FIGURES

Architectural Components Team |

Atkins / Grimshaw / GIA Equation / Maynard

Components |

GFRC cladding ~50'000m2 (approximately the area of 7 full size football pitches)

Platform Edge Screen ~3.8km

Signs

Balustrades & Handrails

Seats

Luminaires

Equipment integration

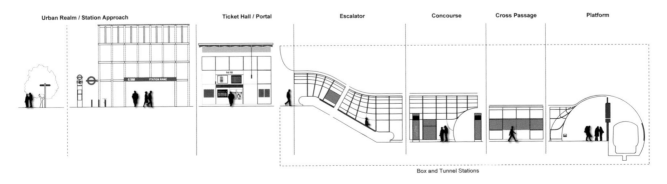

Urban Realm / Station Approach   Ticket Hall / Portal   Escalator   Concourse   Cross Passage   Platform

Box and Tunnel Stations

MODAL IDENTITY
LOCAL IDENTITY

| Generic concourse tunnel design

this was Tottenham Court Road, in another the purple roundel announced merely "Station Name". The exit led you to no ticket hall. Instead you passed through narrow corridors and security-locked doors until you emerged into a large industrial estate. This was Crossrail's prototype testing laboratory.

All the common components that you'll soon become familiar with on the Elizabeth line, were tried out here first, at full scale. Different versions of everything from the passageway linings (in close-fitting glass-reinforced cement or GFRC) to the escalator (finished in stainless steel, incorporating lighting both reflected off the ceiling and illuminating the treads) were brought together here and in some cases made here too.

To begin with mock-ups were used, later moving on to working prototypes from a roster of manufacturers. This way, potential faults could be spotted and ironed out. Nothing was left to chance. Even the invisible bolts that hold together the complex multi-purpose wall separating platform from track were specially designed, and tested by Imperial College to make sure they cannot work loose.

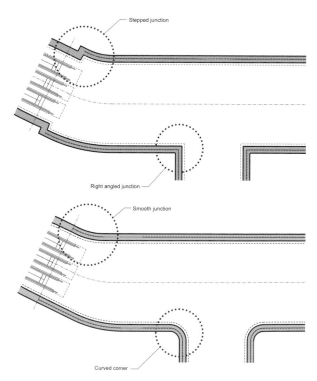

Engineering design concept for the tunnel intersections

Sprayed concrete structural lining

This test station, inside a factory-sized shed, was a hugely valuable asset, helping development of the common parts that unite all the new below-ground stations and feature largely in all the others. Here especially the pale GFRC passageway lining sections were refined to match the engineering concept of 'soft', curved junctions to the broad, tall passageways. These are made possible by the sprayed-concrete construction technique, which allows for fluid forms. There are no sharp angles, the lining pieces fit as closely as possible to the actual tunnel walls, and they are kept clear of clutter. Their design started as a stage set and developed through prototyping of actual pieces, reducing weight and the number of joints required, incorporating acoustic absorption.

While the individual stations and their surroundings are designed to respond to the local context (and in the cases of several outlying stations are themselves historic), these common parts are designed to achieve consistency and familiarity from end to end of the line. This is a proven way of doing things, as shown by the inter-war heyday of the original London Underground. Architects, product and lighting designers worked together in a consortium to achieve a vital aim: simplicity and clarity.

Not for them the confusing visual clutter of dangling signs, train indicators, lighting, loudspeakers and so forth. Instead everything is integrated into the overall architecture of the spaces. The result is cool, restrained, aiming to stand outside fashion. As it has to, being designed to last 125 years. That's not over-ambitious when you consider that London's first underground equivalent, the original Metropolitan line from

| Prototype GFRC panel

Paddington to Farringdon after which all the world's metros are named, is now more than 150 years old and still in full use.

There is a common set of parts – seating, signage, communications and fire safety equipment, handrails, screens, escalators, lifts and so on. This creates a consistent and quickly familiar feel for the line. In the tunnelled stations in central London these components are joined by the curving GFRC passageway linings, the spaces flowing gently into each other.

Reducing clutter to almost nothing requires a high level of design co-ordination. Perhaps the hardest-working part of the whole endeavour are the platform screens. Glazed with sliding doors to match the trains, above door height they contain several bands with various functions including train indicators and route diagrams, PA systems, removable access panels to the electronics, and finally a broad lighting zone. Avoiding separate light fittings, this washes light evenly down the curved cladding to the granite-terrazzo flooring. The upshot is that, looking down the platform, there is no visual confusion. You will normally only see the occasional sideways-projecting sign to mark an exit and that too will be mounted on the platform-edge screen.

| *Full size platform mock-up*

Generic platform tunnel design in mined stations

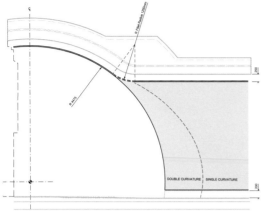

Crosspassage Elevation

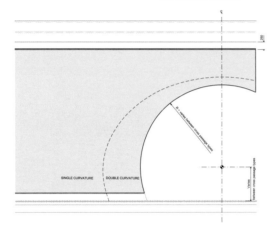

Platform Elevation

IN DETAIL
Curved
tunnel linings
concept and design

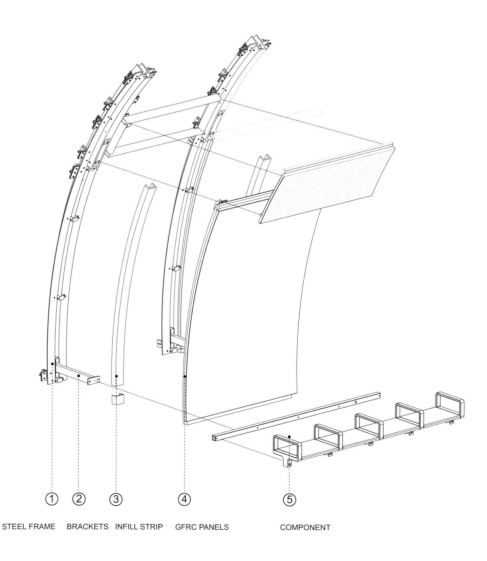

Assembly of cladding system

① STEEL FRAME ② BRACKETS ③ INFILL STRIP ④ GFRC PANELS ⑤ COMPONENT

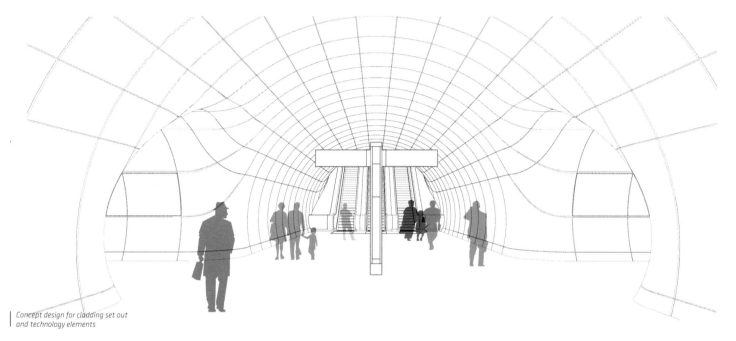

Concept design for cladding set out
and technology elements

Construction of concourse structural lining

IN DETAIL
Curved tunnel linings

prototyping
and testing

| Above left : Form liner for acoustic GFRC panels

| Above right: Construction of GFRC prototype

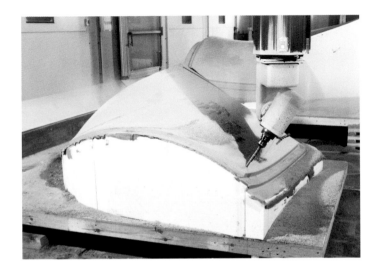

Manufacturing process for GFRC junction panels

LED LUMINAIRE
Uplights located on all internal totems

SPEAKERS & GRILLE
Speakers located behind grille at the corners of the totem. Speakers used on all internal totems

PROJECTING SIGNAGE
Located on totems at tunnel junctions

CLADDING
Glazed panels on all totems

GLAZED SIGNAGE
Hinged panel on all totems for internal access

TAPE BARRIER
Tape barrier on internal totems as required

LV SOCKET
Integrated low voltage socket with hinged stainless steel cover plate for access. Fitted to all internal totems

EDGE TRIM & END CAPS
Stainless steel edge trims and capping plates to all totems.

SKIRTING
Removable stainless steel skirting to all totems

IN DETAIL
Station signage and lighting
a unified approach

Similarly a very old concept has been revived: the free-standing finger-post at concourse junctions. Known as 'totems', these are made possible by the spaciousness of the below-ground concourses and will show the way to the right platform and exit or interchange for you. But these apparently simple devices also throw light up at the ceiling, incorporate loudspeakers for announcements, carry subsidiary information such as local maps, and in some cases have pull-out ribbons for when spaces need to be roped off.

Items you would scarcely glance at, such as handrails, have been rigorously tested. Stainless steel mounting brackets, for instance, have carefully chamfered corners lest small children might occasionally bang their heads. A range of seating includes all-metal types for below ground, but warmer timber seats, sometimes with backs, for above-ground stations. All types have a common clean-design language and are designed to be very tough and long-lasting.

The guiding design principle here is satisfyingly simple. Where you alight or disembark from trains, the environment is controlled right along the line. At street level, the design is more individual, by different architects, responding to the local context. And between the two conditions – for instance in the deep stations where you travel through deep escalator boxes to get to and from platform level – the two types of design imperceptibly move from one to the other.

So you will find common components in the architect-designed ticket halls, and equally it's not unusual to find place-specific design features by individual architects – especially ceiling and lighting designs - finding their way down to platform concourse level. On outlying surface stations, the pre-existing architecture often applies but consistency is supplied by the common components. And that is pretty much it. It's straightforward: but never underestimate just how much design effort goes into making these environments seem effortless.

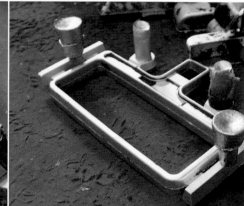

| Above: Casting process for the seat arm rest

| Right: Seat with stainless steel seat pan

IN DETAIL
Seat design
for underground and surface stations

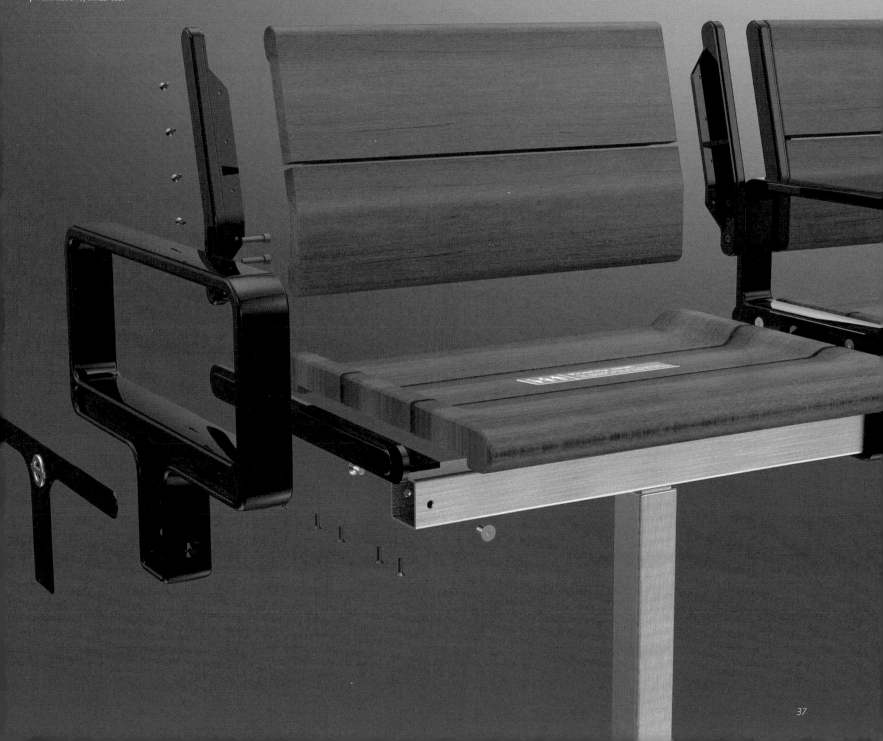

Visualisation of timber seat

Paddington

FACTS & FIGURES

Station structure | **Box**

Excavated material | **315,000 tonnes**

Passenger platform length | **208 metres**

Depth below ground | **20 metres**

Public art | **Cloud Index by Spencer Finch**

Expected passenger numbers
on the Elizabeth line | **174,000 per day**

Number of trains per hour
(peak) | **24 east, 10 west**

"I am going to design, in a great hurry, a station after my own fancy," wrote Isambard Kingdom Brunel to his architect colleague Matthew Digby Wyatt in 1851. This was to be Paddington.

The Crystal Palace – undoubtedly an inspiration for it - was nearing completion in Hyde Park. Typically of Brunel, he trumpeted what a great place the new Paddington Station was going to be and how very good he was but asked for help: "For detail of ornamentation I neither have time nor knowledge, and with all my confidence in my own ability I have never any objection to advice and assistance even in the department which I keep to myself, namely the general design."

Opened in 1854 and now Grade I listed, the London terminus of Brunel's Great Western Railway is one of the world's greatest examples of railway engineering and architecture. He worked not only with Wyatt but also the architect, historian and colour specialist Owen Jones. It's the kind of collaboration that's familiar to us today on large-scale transport projects – without the engineering, the architecture would be impossible and without the architecture, the engineering would be the poorer. Crossrail works on the same engineering-led collaborative principle but the challenge at Paddington was a particularly keen one. Just how do you add a new station to a place that is an acknowledged historic masterpiece?

DESIGN & BUILD

Station architect | **Weston Williamson**

Engineer | **AECOM**

Main contractor | **Costain Skanska JV**

Urban realm designers | **Gillespies / URS / Weston Williamson**

BREEAM Rating | **Very Good**

| *BIM model of Paddington station*

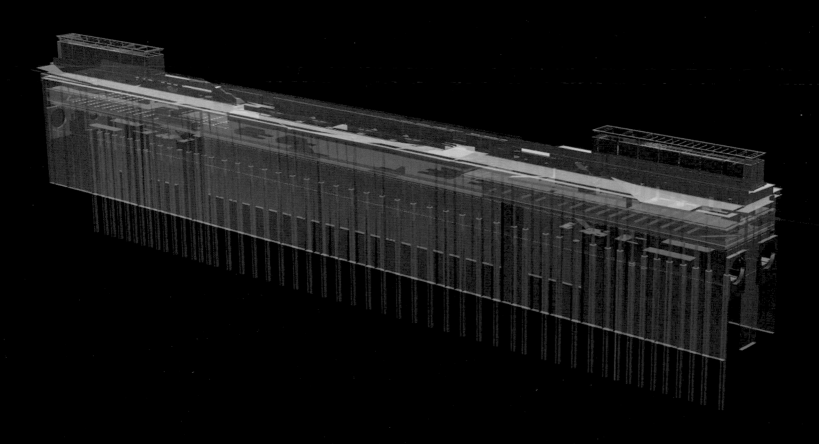

The first big move was made when an earlier version of the Crossrail project was designed at the start of the 1990s. That established the principle that the best place to put the new station was alongside the old station on Eastbourne Terrace, plugging into it below ground level. The architects of the time envisaged opening up the roof to the sky so daylight reached platform concourse level. That proved impractical as envisaged but 20 years later the wholly redesigned station again makes the most of daylight and sky. This, after all, was what Brunel himself did: Paddington Station is sunk into a cutting, with daylight mostly entering from above.

At Paddington, the new station is also a box sunk into the ground, rather than consisting of tunnelled platforms and concourses as is the case in several of the central London stations (and as would have been the case in the 1993 version). It is made possible by the earlier "Paddington Integrated Project" which opened up the north side of the station with a spacious new concourse next to the canal basin at Paddington Waterside, later being joined by a new 15 storey commercial development above. This was part of a general reorganisation of traffic and pedestrian movement around the station – taxis included – to prepare the way for the Crossrail project on the south side.

*Sketch and model of early 'column of light' design
for Paddington's Crossrail station*

Interim public space at Paddington Canal-side

| *Ticket hall at Paddington*

| Taxi concourse at Paddington

| Paddington station

There, where taxis used to arrive and depart beneath a sunken canopy, you once again find a glass canopy, but this time up at street level, longer and wider, serving as a roof for the new station. And what a roof. It is a steel grid 120 metres (nearly 400 feet) long by 20 metres (over 65 feet) wide, its glass shaded by the integral cloudscape artwork of American artist Spencer Finch (titled Cloud Index and funded by Heathrow and the City of London) which will become one of the sights of London. Daylight floods down to Departures Road below – a covered, stone-paved street with informal benches, lined with shops and cafes on the station side, that is a destination in itself. From there you can walk on the level into the mainline station, descend the escalators to Elizabeth line platform level, interchange with buses and taxis or just walk on your way in comfort.

Building alongside the old station like this gives Paddington an expanded presence while leaving the mothership intact. Far from trying to compete with it, it is in a different, cooler architectural language that nonetheless replicates the rigorous 10-foot grid-pattern of Brunel's 1854 building. Everything is scaled up or down from that module, which means that all the components of the new station down to the dished precast concrete ceiling coffers containing 'lily pad' circular light fittings make a coherent family of parts derived from Brunel's imperial measurements.

For the rail user, this is the single most dramatic sequence of spaces on the system. Uniquely, it is a station you will be able to look down into from the street, which also contains

two large pavilions housing the ventilation gear – for once freestanding rather than concealed inside other buildings. These are sizeable pieces of architecture in their own right. As you descend into the station via lift or escalator, the station box is lined with flush-jointed brick, perforated in places for acoustic absorption. Other materials are equally durable: glass, bronze and anodised aluminium, plus the stainless steel of the common components such as the escalators. Smooth elliptical columns, bronze-clad to head height, carry the weight of the structure.

Outside on Eastbourne Terrace, buses come and go, taxis drop people off, there are bike and motorcycle stands and wide zebra crossings to make access easy. New benches, trees and paving help to create a new sense of place and ease transit for those on foot.

It is remarkable that Brunel's station of 1854 should have finally – though with great difficulty - proved adaptable to vastly increased passenger numbers. It has been achieved by sensitively expanding the station with its Tube and Elizabeth line links to both north and south while leaving the original building standing proud. This, combined with the new public realm, associated building developments and the canal corridor on the north side, have made it a much more open and accessible place. It will also be less busy, given that many more people will now pass right through on the Elizabeth line rather than changing onto other lines. That will give everyone more time and space to tip their hats to the original engineering and frankly eccentric architecture of Brunel, Wyatt and Jones.

| *Northern entrance to Paddington*

| *Platforms at Paddington*

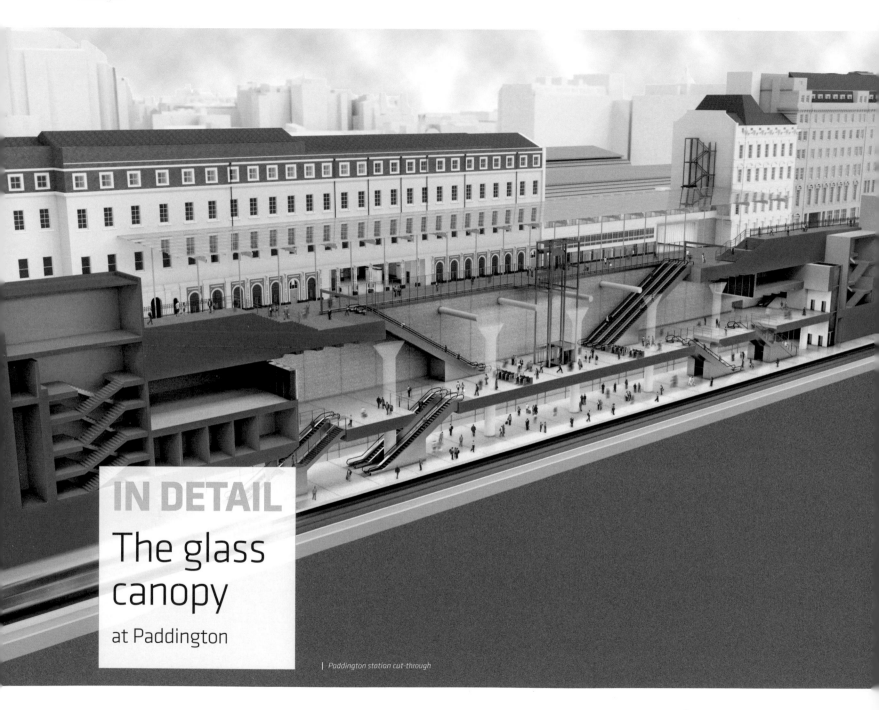

IN DETAIL
The glass
canopy
at Paddington

| Paddington station cut-through

Existing Paddington station and
new station to the south

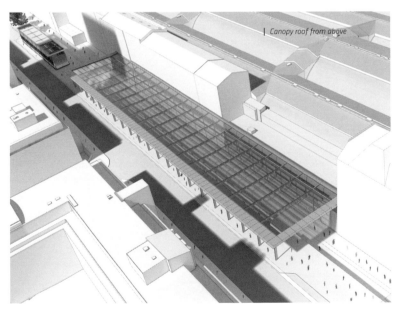

Canopy roof from above

Visual of A Cloud Index by Spencer Finch

Bond Street

FACTS & FIGURES

Station structure | **Mined**

Excavated material | **302,000 tonnes**

Passenger platform length | **255 metres (westbound) 249 metres (eastbound)**

Depth below ground | **28 metres**

Expected passenger numbers on the Elizabeth line (daily) | **137,000**

No. of trains (peak, each way) | **24**

Bond Street is one of London's mysteries – there is no street of that exact name, despite what the Monopoly Board suggests. There is an Old Bond Street and a New Bond Street but neither the existing tube station nor its new companion is on either of these. This tells you that "Bond Street" is really a district, a subdivision of Mayfair.

The new station here is also very London in the way it slots into a dense urban grain, just south of and parallel to Oxford Street. This relieves the crowding on Oxford Street by drawing people a little way south.

| *Ticket hall at Hanover Square, Bond Street*

| *1990s design by Allies and Morrison for the Bond Street ticket hall at Hanover-Square*

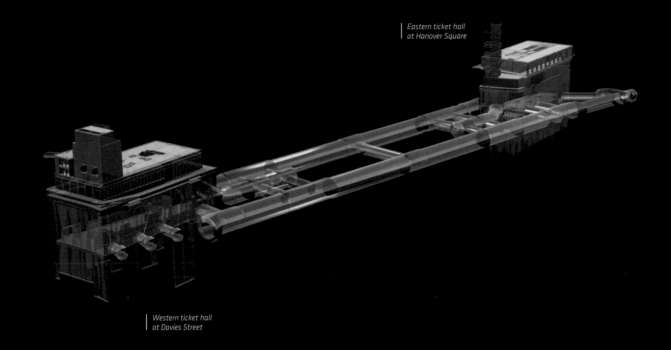

| Eastern ticket hall
at Hanover Square

| Western ticket hall
at Davies Street

DESIGN & BUILD

Station architect | **John McAslan + Partners**

Engineer | **WSP**

Main contractor | **Costain Skanska JV**

Urban realm designs | **John McAslan + Partners / WPS / Publica**

Oversite development partners | **Great Portland Estates (Hanover Square), Grosvenor Estates (Davies Street)**

BREEAM Rating | **Very Good**

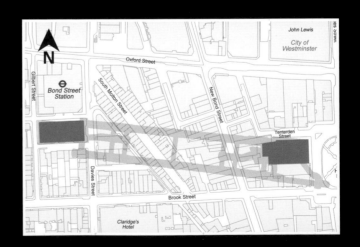

Its western entrance – connecting below ground to Central and Jubilee lines at the much-upgraded Tube station - is on redbrick Davies Street. Its eastern entrance is in stately Hanover Square which is close to Oxford Circus, but a very different, calmer world. Hanover Square, being very large and central, is what made the excavation alongside it feasible. It had become a rather neglected space in the past but, once the Elizabeth line is operational, it will be the subject of a significant urban realm project that will make it and the streets around it a considerably more agreeable place than before. It forms part of an extensive streetscape improvement plan with Westminster Council which will connect through to another nearby grand but under-used public space with improvement plans, Cavendish Square to the north of the stores on Oxford Street.

The architects have taken a modern-classical approach, giving both of their station entrance buildings broad portals flanked by colonnades – red sandstone and bronze for Davies Street, pale Portland stone for Hanover Square. The beams of the coffered ceilings link the lines of columns.

| *Bond Street eastern ticket hall*

The buildings above the station entrances – which as with all the 'oversite developments' contribute to the cost of the line and which will invisibly contain air vent shafts - will pick up on this restrained, post-and-beam aesthetic. Not only does the Hanover Square development bring eight floors of residential, office and retail space, but it adds to Crossrail's forecourt improvements with a new public courtyard and enhancements to the square.

Entrance at Davies Street with office development above

Entrance at Hanover Square with residential, office and retail development above

Descent to the tunnel concourse from Bond Street western ticket hall

Anatomy of a ticket hall

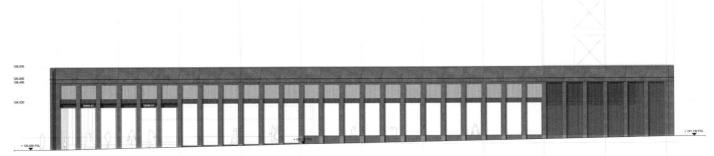

West Facade - Gilbert Street

North Facade - Weighouse Street

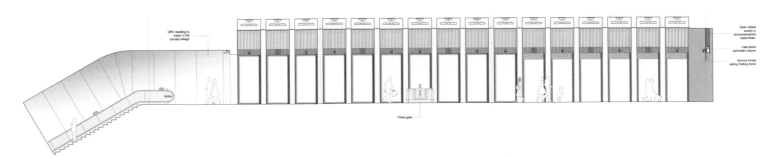

GRC cladding to match C100 concept design

Open ribbed screen in bronze/anodized metal finish.

Cast stone perimeter column

Bronze tinned sliding folding doors

Ticket gate

Everything is kept well-proportioned and elegant, with a dash of upmarket glitz appropriate for the shops round here. Both buildings feature tall bronze hinged grille doors between their columns which can fold shut to close the station off for the few hours it is not running. Inside the ticket halls, you find other choice details such as fluted bronze columns. The bronze re-emerges as cladding for kiosks, walls and – in perforated form – providing acoustic absorption for the larger spaces. It is used in sculptural relief form on the ceiling of the escalator box leading down to the intermediate western concourse which connects across to the tube station. The descent through these spaces is quite grand – there is something of a Moscow-metro feel. From there on down you move into the more familiar realm of the line-wide platform-concourse components, including the smooth pale concourse linings with gently curving 'bellmouth' corners.

The existing Bond Street Tube station, hitherto a confusing and awkward place to use, is being hugely upgraded by London Underground to handle all the extra passengers once it is connected to the Elizabeth line. Like all of the stations on the new route, it will become fully accessible via lifts to all levels.

So below-ground interchange passengers will account for a large proportion of the station's users. But for the full experience, come to the surface. There's an enduring quality to the new Bond Street station, playing off the context of upmarket stores, art galleries and apartment blocks round here. Dare we say it's just a bit glamorous?

| *Hanover Square at night*

| *Bond Street eastern ticket hall*

CASE STUDY Partnership at Hanover Square

The entrance onto Hanover Square is topped by a new development which, in a building extending onto adjacent sites, will provide 325,000 square feet of new homes, offices and shops.

The collaboration between Crossrail, Great Portland Estates and Westminster Council has meant the building – which will serve as a local landmark for the railway – echoes the colonnades and Portland stone of the station's design. The surrounding public area will be improved by generous pedestrian areas, new diagonal crossings across the square, new public courtyard and improved surfacing, seating and lighting.

Station entrance and residential, office and retail development above at Hanover Square

Hanover Square

New pedestrian plaza at Hanover Square

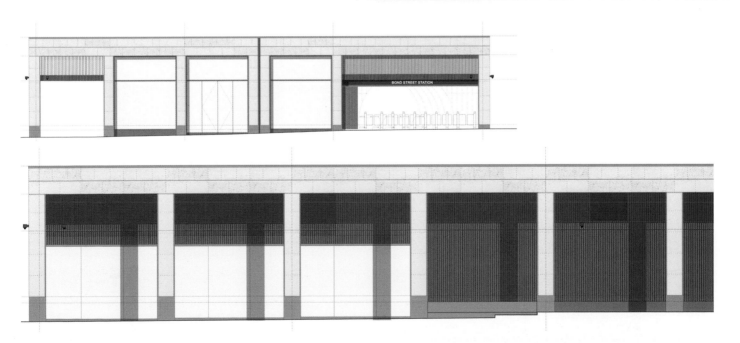

BOND STREET STATION

Tottenham Court Road

FACTS & FIGURES

Station structure | **Mined**

Passenger platform length | **234 metres**

Depth below ground | **24 metres**

Public art | **Gold leaf ceiling by Richard Wright. Exquisite Corpse by Douglas Gordon**

Expected passenger numbers on the Elizabeth line (daily) | **170,000**

No. of trains per hour (peak, each way) | **24**

Perhaps the single most noticeable piece of the Crossrail project – because of the way it happens at a key central London crossroads, with inevitable impact on buildings and traffic - is Tottenham Court Road.

Stretching nearly a kilometre from a new plaza in front of the listed Centre Point tower westwards to Dean Street in Soho, it runs right beneath Soho Square. Further complexity is added by the fact that this is a prime interchange station, connecting to Northern and Central lines. The existing Underground station at the crossroads was the first to be improved, the previously cramped ticket hall made six times larger, new banks of escalators installed and new entrances built.

| *Tottenham Court Road ticket hall at Dean Street*

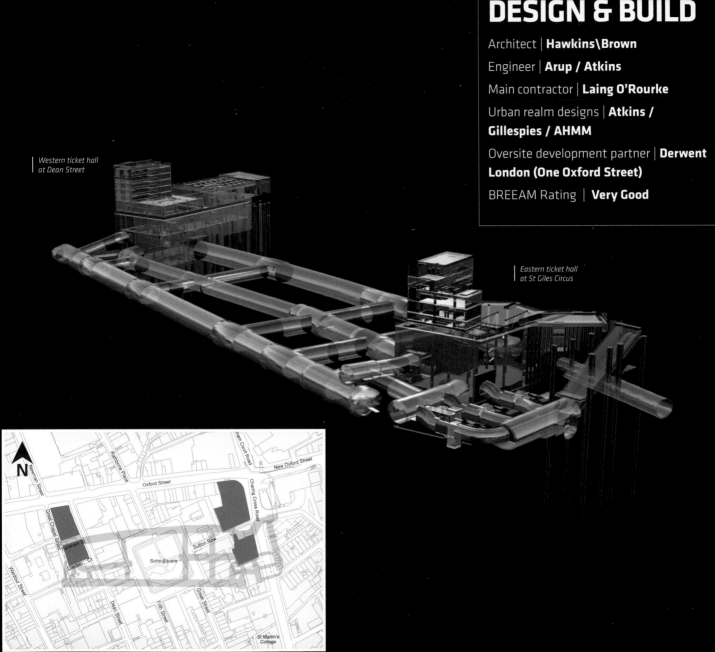

Western ticket hall at Dean Street

Eastern ticket hall at St Giles Circus

N

Newman Street

Rathbone Place

Oxford Street

New Oxford Street

Charing Cross Road

Great Chapel Street

Fareham St

Diadem Ct

Wardour Street

Soho Square

Sutton Row

Dean Street

Frith Street

Greek Street

St Martin's College

The 230 metre-plus length of the platforms means that – in common with many of the central London stations – there are two widely-spaced ticket halls, depending on which end you choose to emerge from. The eastern 'daytime' end gives you the modernist totem of Centre Point plus shopping and theatreland, the western 'night-time' end is in the more intimate world of Soho. The station is designed accordingly – the eastern light and open, the western darker and more mysterious in black and gold. Striking new asymmetrical glass-and-steel canopy entrances form part of a new landscape in the Centre Point plaza. This is a vital piece of new urban realm to help absorb the 200,000 or so people expected to use the station once the Elizabeth line opens – a 50 per cent increase. Previously Centre Point was on a relatively inaccessible island. In Soho, a single escalator drop takes you directly from the hubbub of Soho life at street level to the platforms, filtering daylight into the dark.

| Glazed canopy entrance at St Giles Circus

Ticket hall at Dean Street reflects the area's night-time economy

IN DETAIL

Local context
at Tottenham
Court Road

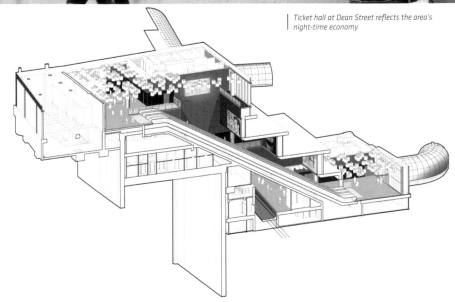

The colour scheme at the platform-level concourse at St Giles reflects daytime shopping and theatreland

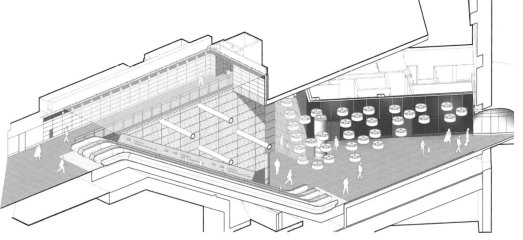

| Daniel Buren art work, integrated ticket hall

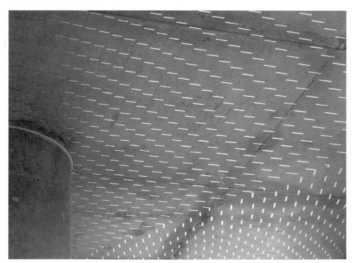

| Applied gold-leaf artwork by Richard Wright

Even at train level, Tottenham Court Road will feel different given that one of the platforms is set out on a unique long curve dictated by the track alignment. But also vital to the feel of the place is the integrated art. This has some history – the Tube station was refurbished with colourful integrated mosaics by sculptor Eduardo Paolozzi back in 1984. 95% of these remain, now restored though some – notably his arched entrance pieces to the escalators from the ticket hall – had to be removed in the expansion because the place they were sited no longer exists. These pieces are also to be restored and displayed at the University of Edinburgh, where Paolozzi studied and taught and which already has a large collection of his work.

The tradition established by Paolozzi continues nearby with new integrated artworks by French artist Daniel Buren at the eastern end, commissioned by London Underground. His monochrome diamonds lead you to Oxford Street, while his coloured circles take you to theatreland.

Next came the commissions, which will make this the richest station for art on the network. An applied gold-leaf artwork by Turner Prize-winning Richard Wright will form the ceiling of one of the eastern escalator boxes. At the western, Soho, the artwork of Douglas Gordon, a fellow Turner winner, will be represented.

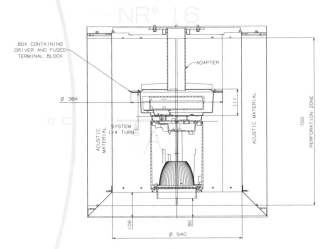

A distinctive architectural feature of Tottenham Court Road is the way the architects have designed 'drum' light fittings overhead which incorporate acoustic absorbers to keep down noise and echo.

Acoustic lighting drum
at Tottenham Court Road

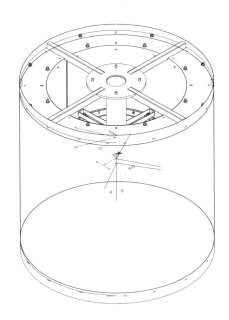

Intended to reference theatre-style lighting, the drums are set between the deep roof beams and present from platform-level lobbies to street-level ticket halls, they are as much of a station identifier as the artworks. You'll know when you reach Tottenham Court Road.

Station entrance and residential and office development at Dean Street

As the station completes at both ends, the scars of construction are healed by new buildings above. At the eastern end these include offices and shops plus a new 500-seat theatre – replacement for a local landmark live-music venue that had to go to make way for the construction works, the Astoria. The two main new buildings step aside

IN DETAIL
Supplier snapshot
at Tottenham Court Road

Across the Crossrail project, 95% of contracts have been awarded to companies in the United Kingdom, 65% outside of London, spreading the economic benefit of the project across the UK.

slightly to create another new piece of public realm leading from the Centre Point plaza to Soho Square past the redbrick church of St. Barnabas.

Meanwhile the western end will be rebuilt with residential blocks, appropriate for the more domestic scale and tradition of Soho. Enhanced by pedestrianizing the tip of Dean Street, the flow of people through to Oxford Street will be markedly easier. The one right over the station entrance will be by the same architects, Hawkins/Brown, and in the same black-and-gold aesthetic. Overall, the economic impact of the combined development above and below ground has already transformed a much loved corner of London, over a surprisingly large area.

1) Black reconstituted stone cladding with projecting window reveals

2) Recessed pleated gold anodised patterned aluminium spandrel panels

3) Recessed frameless glazing with opaque glazed spandrel panel below

4) Pleated gold anodised cladding to balcony interiors

  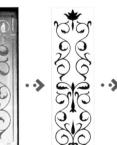 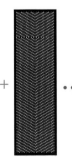  

CASE STUDY An early radical concept for Soho

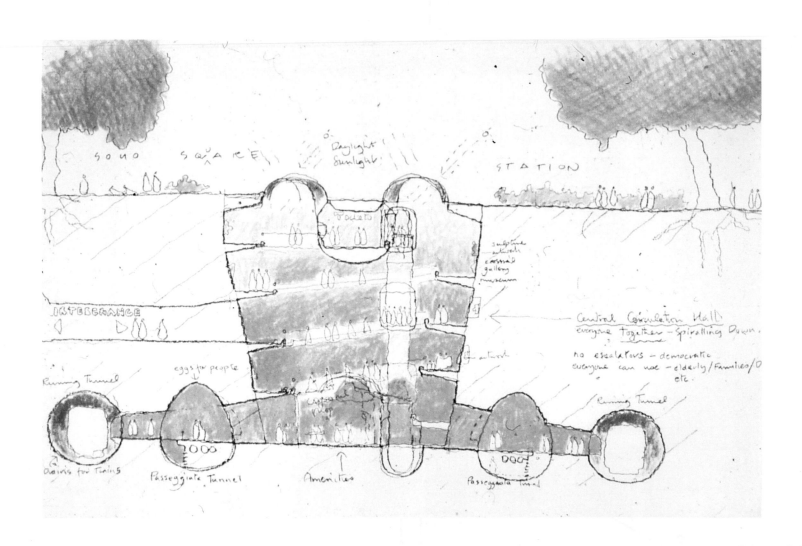

An early 1990s plan by Ralph Erskine and BDP for a centralised station at Tottenham Court Road featured a huge downwards-tapering circulation hall with glazed roof domes, bang in the middle of Soho Square. There was a logic and undoubted verve to this, but it proved impractical. The square remains undisturbed, with the added benefit of pedestrian streetscape improvements at its eastern end.

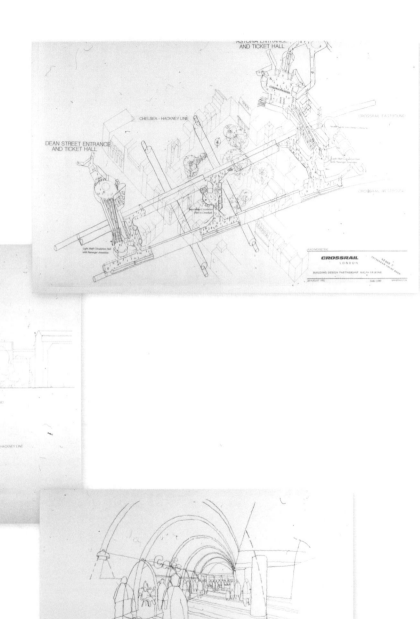

VIEW OF PASSENGER CROSS CONNECTIONS BETWEEN EASTBOUND AND WESTBOUND CONCOURSES

Farringdon

FACTS & FIGURES

Station structure | **Mined**

Excavated material | **306,640 tonnes**

Passenger platform length | **244 metres**

Depth below ground | **30 metres**

Expected passenger numbers on the
Elizabeth line (daily) | **82,000**

No. of trains per hour
(peak, each way) | **24**

Few parts of London have changed so much in recent years as Farringdon, once a light-industrial area handy for the night porters of nearby Smithfield Market and the jewellers of Hatton Garden, now the centre of the Clerkenwell creative industries district.

Hard on the heels of this regeneration came transport improvements. First Thameslink came through to add to the old Metropolitan line, and now Crossrail will add the Elizabeth line. This is the only place on the network where the new East-West railway intersects with the much-upgraded north-south railway. With such connections, it's no wonder that property developers are piling into Farringdon and its surrounding area. This required a substantial station that is also appropriate for the historic, diverse character of the area on the banks of what was the River Fleet.

| *Interchange concourse, Farringdon*

DESIGN & BUILD

Architect | **Aedas**

Engineer | **AECOM**

Main contractor | **Bam Ferrovial Kier JV**

Urban realm designs | **Burns + Nice / URS**

Oversite development partner | **Cardinal Lysander (Cardinal House)**

BREEAM Rating | **Very Good**

Eastern ticket hall at Long Lane

Western ticket hall at Cowcross Street

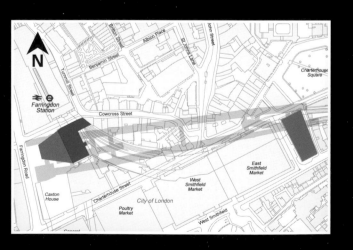

"Breakfast at Tiffany's", the film starring Audrey Hepburn, might seem an unlikely inspiration but it's one cited by the architects because of Hatton Garden: we can all gaze at the jewels in the window while clutching our breakfast coffee and nibbling a pastry. That's the cue for the western interchange ticket hall: the eastern end, which surfaces at the far end of Smithfield Market, looks beyond it to the metal-bashing trades of the area and the virtuoso heavyweight concrete of the Barbican complex. End to end, it's a contrast between strength and delicacy.

The western end is the dominant one, expected to handle around 80% of passengers. Plenty of preparatory work took place first. The Underground station has added a secondary northern entrance and ticket hall to cope with increased passenger flows to and from Clerkenwell. To the south, a Thameslink ground level ticket hall is already operational, directly across the street from the main existing 1930s Underground entrance. This large new hall will handle Elizabeth line passengers, via an interchange hall a level lower to the west. From there you descend to platform level. Next to it, a new eight storey development will house retail and office space for the area.

| Ticket hall at Charterhouse Street

| Integrated ticket hall at Cowcross Street

Back inside the station, the two lines diverge at the western end, and the angle between them generates the look and feel of the structure around you as you descend into the station. Very large precast concrete roof sections are arranged in diamond pattern (again recalling Hatton Garden). Modelled to lighten their appearance, they also inspire a diamond pattern to walls, done in glass and a light golden stainless steel. The walls to the escalator boxes use the same subtly-patterned materials, plus at high level perforated light golden stainless steel panel to absorb noise.

Your descent (or ascent) takes you through two broad wedge-shaped spaces or apses which, along with the structural geometry, serve to alter perspective: this gives the spaces – well daylit from above, with indirect lighting taking over further down – a greater sense of depth. It might not exactly be Tiffany's, but there is something of the upmarket shop window about all this.

At the eastern end of the station beyond Smithfield, things are just as sophisticated but more straightforward. There is an innovation however: the lifts here move on a slope rather than vertically. At ticket hall level, it's all about concrete and iron – a deep coffered concrete roof supporting the building that will appear above filled with offices and shops, and heavy metal sliding-screen gates. These can be pulled out to enclose the open entrance corner, or slide back behind glass walls so they remain in view. Their design is derived from a barcode saying "Farringdon" – an in-joke only robots would read. Light gold stainless steel reappears as a perforated acoustic layer in the ceiling coffers. Indeed, some slightly glitzy touches appear even at platform level, the patterning and rich materials sparingly used among the common components.

Outside the ticket halls, street level improvements extend quite some way into the surrounding city, an important part of Crossrail's integrated design approach. Here the challenge is to handle the increased footfall in the area. A public pedestrian-priority plaza appears between the two ticket halls – joining Thameslink, the Elizabeth line and Underground - at the western end of Cowcross Street. From there a central line of trees and seating leads to Farringdon Road, where the pedestrian crossing will continue across at the same level. This corner will be enlivened by cafes. The eastern ticket hall on Long Lane beyond Smithfield Market will benefit from traffic calming, widened footways in York stone, and a surface of granite setts in Hayne Street (now pedestrian priority) which runs into Charterhouse Square.

View down Lindsey Street

Entrance at
Cowcross Street

Precast concrete soffit

30mm x 30mm recess in beam

Hybrid structure made from steel beams encased in precast concrete

Emergency lighting in nodes

In-situ concrete soffit

100mm x 50mm recess

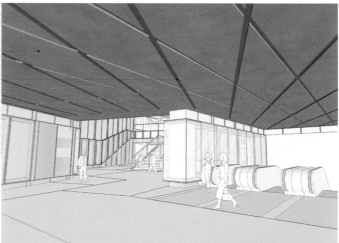

IN DETAIL
Walls and ceilings

in Farringdon's Western Ticket Hall

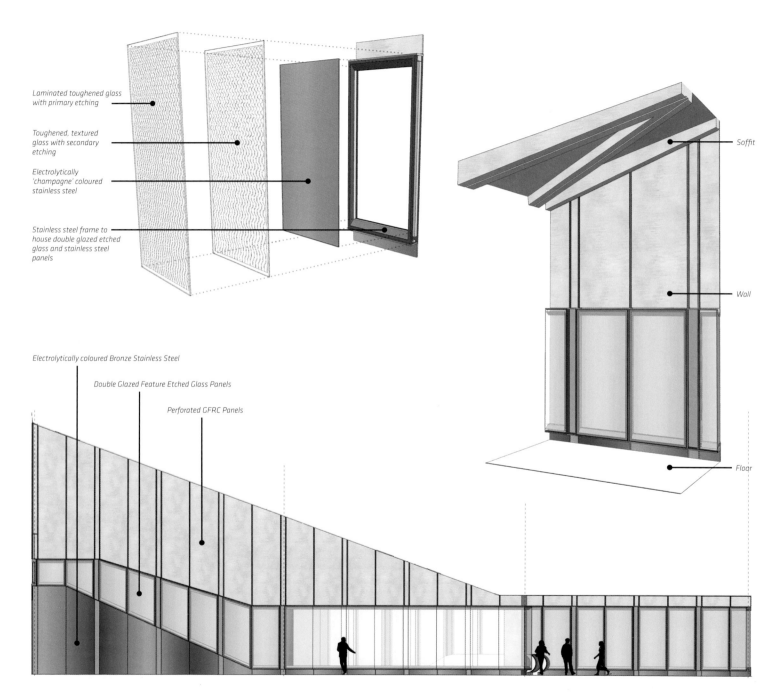

Laminated toughened glass with primary etching

Toughened, textured glass with secondary etching

Electrolytically 'champagne' coloured stainless steel

Stainless steel frame to house double glazed etched glass and stainless steel panels

Soffit

Wall

Floor

Electrolytically coloured Bronze Stainless Steel

Double Glazed Feature Etched Glass Panels

Perforated GFRC Panels

*Precast concrete soffit for
Cowcross Street, Farringdon*

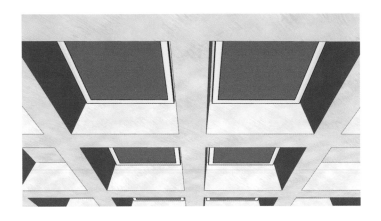

| Barbican ceiling

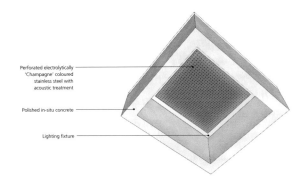

Perforated electrolytically 'Champagne' coloured stainless steel with acoustic treatment

Polished in-situ concrete

Lighting fixture

IN DETAIL
Walls and ceilings

in Farringdon's Eastern Ticket Hall

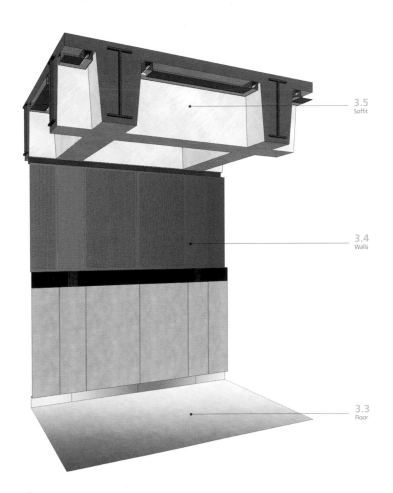

3.5 Soffit

3.4 Walls

3.3 Floor

The deep coffered ceiling of Farringdon's Eastern Ticket Hall. To the left, the inclined lift which follows the escalators to and from the trains

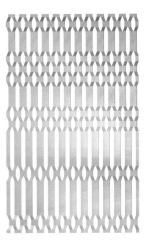

Detailed elevation of gate

Solid when viewed from Charterhouse Street

Transparent when viewed from Long Lane

Liverpool Street

FACTS & FIGURES

Station structure | **Mined**

Excavated material | **567,000 tonnes**

Passenger platform length | **238 metres**

Depth below ground | **34 metres**

Expected passenger numbers on the
Elizabeth line (daily) | **124,000**

No. of trains per hour (peak, each way) | **24**

Arguably this is the central London station that is most of itself, with the most unified aesthetic from end to end – despite the fact that each end connects to a different existing station, the west in Moorgate and the east, Liverpool Street.

A striking geometric motif that runs right through it, from the ceilings of the ticket halls to the walls of the escalator boxes. If you can imagine a modernist take on Art Deco, then perhaps this is it. In the constant churn of redevelopment of the City of London at this point, with buildings being demolished and rebuilt all round it, the station will provide its own, distinctive voice.

Upper escalator with inclined lift from
Broadgate ticket hall

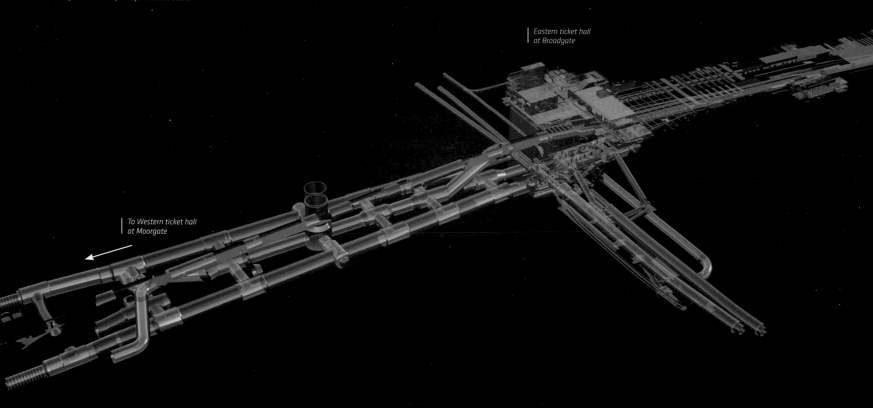

BIM model of Liverpool Street station

Eastern ticket hall at Broadgate

To Western ticket hall at Moorgate

DESIGN & BUILD

Architect | **Wilkinson Eyre**

Engineer | **Mott MacDonald**

Main contractor | **Laing O'Rourke**

Urban realm designs | **Burns + Nice / URS**

Oversite development partner | **Aviva Investors**

BREEAM Rating | **Very Good**

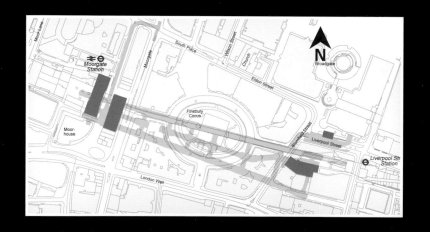

The archaeology was what made the headlines during the early construction phase, however. There were four main layers of it, right where the eastern ticket hall was being dug. Beneath a layer of Victorian foundations - including those of Broad Street Station which vanished under redevelopment in the 1980s - came the Bedlam burial site, including a mass burial from the Great Plague of 1665. Beneath that was the medieval area known as Moorfields Marsh, and finally – six metres down – evidence of Roman suburbs along a road out of the city. All of this was carefully excavated and recorded by archaeologists: it is rare that such an extensive opportunity to explore the capital's past occurs. Crossrail also has to dodge a maze of

Liverpool Street station
underground cross section

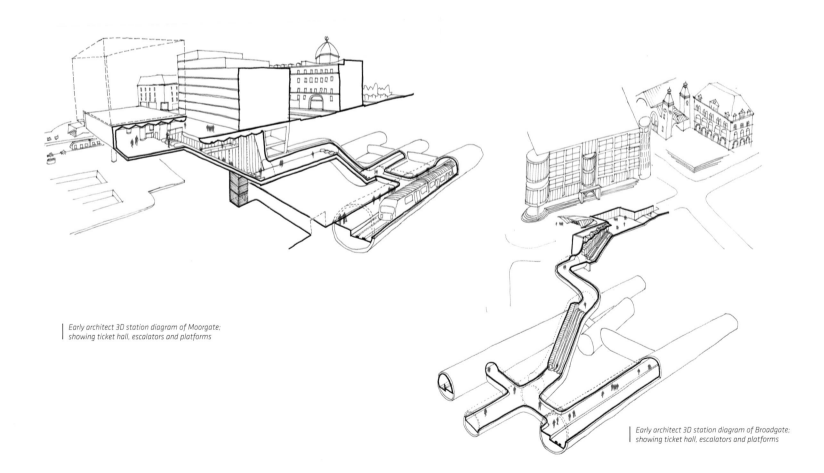

Early architect 3D station diagram of Moorgate;
showing ticket hall, escalators and platforms

Early architect 3D station diagram of Broadgate;
showing ticket hall, escalators and platforms

sewers and existing tube lines including the abandoned Post Office railway. The combined constraints make the station here one of the trickiest to thread into the urban fabric.

The western end connects to the existing Moorgate Underground and Great Northern station, while the eastern end links through to the Liverpool Street mainline terminus and Central line. Between the two lies Finsbury Circus, lined by massive largely interwar buildings and big enough to have tree-lined gardens at its centre – London's first public park, dating back to 1606. These gardens and the streetscape of the Circus will be restored once the work is complete, with lawns, borders and a new café for the locals. It is the second time the Circus has been excavated – the considerably shallower Metropolitan and Circle line, built in the 1870s, passes directly beneath it, end to end.

At the Moorgate end, an above-ground ticket hall on Moorfields also provides the base for a new commercial building above, 65 metres wide, so the design makes use of that width with a broad portal entrance, where angled blue glass walls channel passengers in and out. Escalators and steps run up the side to the Barbican's 'highwalk' podium level, while new high-quality paving in keeping with the City's own materials provides much more pedestrian space on a revived Moorfields, linking through north and south to existing piazzas.

At the eastern, Liverpool Street station end, the ticket hall is below a new landscaped plaza paved in York stone, part of the

| Ticket hall at Broadgate

*Station entrance and office development
at Moorfields*

extensive urban realm works that complete the project and link through to the Broadgate development immediately to the north.

A glazed-wedge canopy, five metres high, takes you down to the eastern ticket hall, its stainless steel portals behind the glass bunched and pleated, concertina fashion. Other connections will be from within the existing mainline/tube interchange. The architectural language of the interior spaces at both ends is the same, driven by the need to maximise their height: a shallow geometric ceiling treatment made from precast reinforced concrete with the sparkle of mica in it. The intersecting angles of these ceilings, extending from ticket halls into the escalator boxes, make a rhythm, visually

Glazed canopy entrance and urban realm
at Broadgate

IN DETAIL

Geometric ceiling

in Liverpool Street's ticket halls

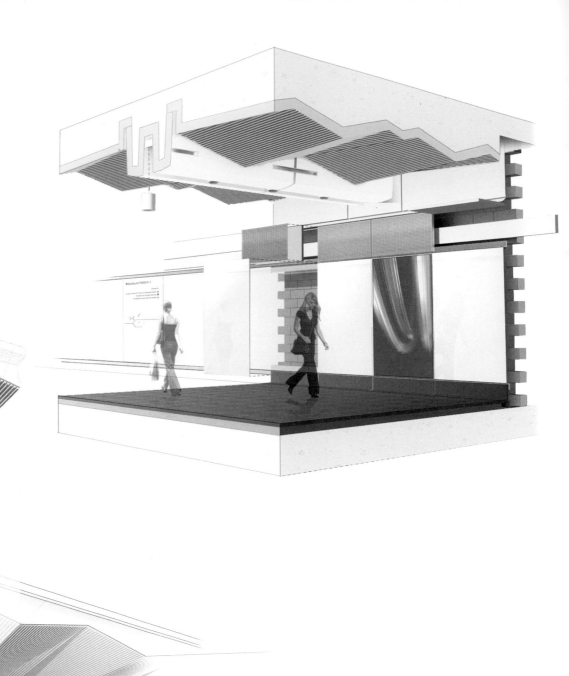

Ticket hall at Moorgate

changing as you move beneath it. Some see a subliminal reference to City pinstripes in the texture, but what most of us will get out of these spaces is a sense of clarity and dynamism: the grooved, angled ceilings help with the acoustics and glow with indirect lighting.

Back-painted glass and stainless steel are the wall materials of choice for the ticket halls. Descending the escalator boxes, the geometric treatment continues in a different vein in the patterning on the walls. This gives a visual texture to what are otherwise flat surfaces. Blue glass appears again in the sides of the escalators, and from there you are into the tunnelled realm of spacious platform concourses.

In summary, Liverpool Street is all about expressing space, light and movement.

Whitechapel

FACTS & FIGURES

Station structure | **Mined**

Excavated material | **451,000 tonnes**

Passenger platform length | **240 metres**

Depth below ground | **30 metres**

Expected passenger numbers on the
Elizabeth line (daily) | **99,000**

No. of trains per hour (peak, each way) | **24**

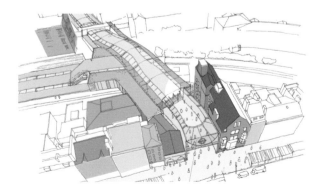

| *Ticket hall at Whitechapel*

While there is ambition to the scale, quality and passenger experience of the new railway, there is no one formula to the design of the new stations, beyond the use of certain materials and designed components – seating, signage, and so on - shared across the system.

Circumstances are different at each location, different communities demanding different responses. Whitechapel is a total one-off because here, right behind the historic, busy Whitechapel Road with its market – once the manor of gangsters the Krays - is where the Elizabeth line will intersect with two other lines and some unique Victorian engineering.

The north-south Overground in its brick cutting runs beneath the east-west Underground while the new tunnels sweep through slightly to the north at a deeper level. How to reconcile all this and make pedestrian links in the hinterland to the north with its school, sports centre and housing? The response is to run a new station concourse from the High Street, along the line of the Overground cutting via a new mezzanine route. From there you drop down via banks

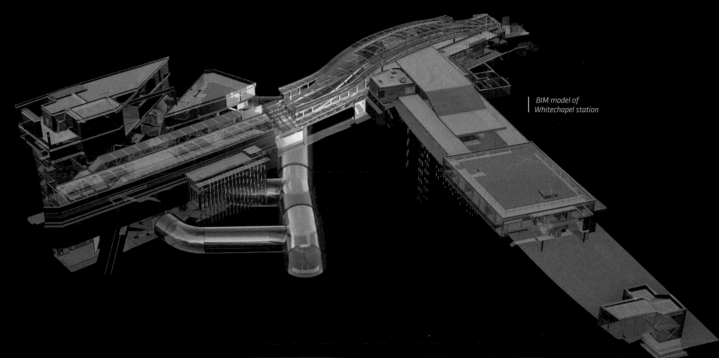

*BIM model of
Whitechapel station*

DESIGN & BUILD

Architect | **BDP**

Engineer | **Arcadis**

Main contractor | **BBMV JV**

Urban realm designs | **BDP / Arcadis**

BREEAM Rating | **Very Good**

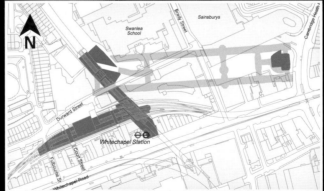

Overground platforms and suspended walkway at Whitechapel

of escalators and lifts to each of the three lines. Achieving this simple solution, with the two old lines remaining in use, required design ingenuity of a high order.

The raised concourse – think of it as an undulating covered bridge – perches within the Overground cutting, supported off its brick arches via steel struts. It floats in the space, allowing daylight down to the Overground platforms. Its 'green' roof, topped with carbon-cleansing sedum plants, dips down under a new road bridge connecting Durward Street behind. This plus the re-use of existing materials helps give the station a "very good" score in the BREEAM sustainability

| View of new Whitechapel concourse from below

method. Escalators down to the Elizabeth line platform at the northern end are placed in a diagonal slice through the western vent shaft building. Bell foundries used to exist round here: patterning to the precast concrete lining to the escalator hall is based on a notation of bell resonance.

All this is mostly hidden from view externally, behind the existing refurbished modest Victorian station frontage on the High Street, enhanced by the widened and stone-paved forecourt, with a new concourse behind it. It is calculated that about 20 per cent of passengers will enter and leave there, the rest interchanging between lines within the station. The most prominent of the new buildings does not handle passengers at all, being the vent and escape shaft on Cambridge Heath Road to the east. That is clad in a "wrap" of bronze, wood and brick. New housing is planned on part of the station site as part of the Borough's masterplan inspired by the new station. This is made possible by the way the station mezzanine concourse design spans a railway rather than using land around it. And beneath it all, the Elizabeth line platforms will be familiar from the rest of the line in their use of smooth cladding with gentle curves, and the common family of signage and seating.

The wider urban setting is well served here, as part of an overall masterplan to improve the area. A public footway runs right through the station from end to end, separate from the concourse. This reconnects people north of the station with the High Street, decreasing walking times to the station and local amenities. Also to the north, a landscaped public square will replace what is at present just a surface car park. To the west, the little Court Street, leading to a pedestrian bridge over the Underground tracks, is made vehicle-fee, better paved and lit to be more welcoming, To the south, the widened pavement on Whitechapel Road acquires something of a boulevard feel, linking across to the former Royal London Hospital, now to be council offices with a new square behind. The station thus becomes part of a new civic focus centre.

| Forecourt at Whitechapel

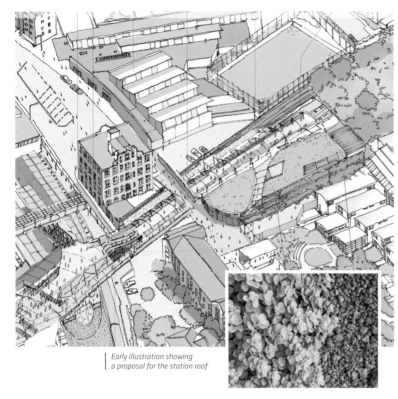

*Early illustration showing
a proposal for the station roof*

*The proposed 'green' roof,
topped with carbon-
cleansing sedum plants*

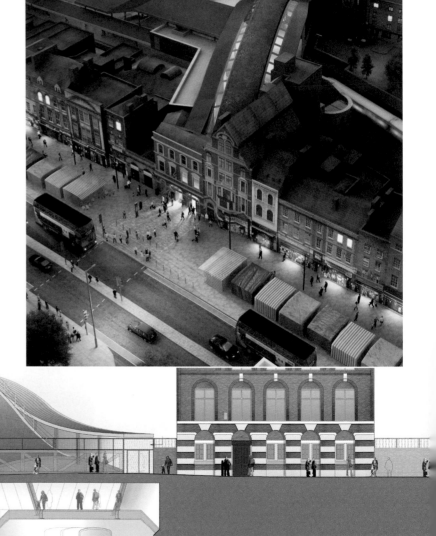

IN DETAIL

Sedum
roof &
entrance

at Whitechapel

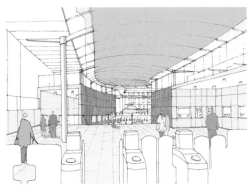

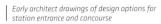

Early architect drawings of design options for station entrance and concourse

Canary Wharf

FACTS & FIGURES

Station structure | **Box**

Passenger platform length | **241 metres**

Depth below ground | **28 metres**

Public art | **Digital art by Michal Rovner**

Expected passenger numbers on the
Elizabeth line (daily) | **68,000**

No. of trains per hour
(peak, each way) | **12**

In a world of verticality, Canary Wharf's Elizabeth line station is a horizontal riposte. If you laid the tallest tower here, 1 Canada Square, on its side, it would still be 74 metres short: the Shard, however, is exactly as tall as this building is long – 310 metres or 1,017 feet. And of course what you see rising above the water of the dock here, like a moored cruise ship, is just part of it. The station box descends way beneath the bottom of the dock. It is the ultimate basement excavation.

The working station slots into both ends of the building, diving into its lower levels via eight escalators clad in yellow glass. The entrance portals lead from one side of the building to the other. From them you descend to the main concourse three levels below ground, thence down again to platform level. The design is conceived to emphasise the journey from light to a darker environment, with materials chosen to contrast with the yellow light filtering down to the escalators in the centre of the space. Walls and lift shafts are clad in extruded pale terracotta and the effect reflects the wider aesthetic of the

| *Platforms at Canary Wharf*

DESIGN & BUILD

Client | **Canary Wharf Contractors Limited**

Station concept architect | **Tony Meadows Associates**

Executive architect | **Adamson Associates**

Oversite development architect | **Foster and Partners**

Engineer and lead consultant | **Arup**

Urban realm design | **Gillespies**

BREEAM Rating | **Very Good**

estate clean, modern, efficient. A digital public art commission will form part of these interiors, in tune with Canary Wharf's overall art-commissioning programme.

From outside, it is all about the roof, wrapping round the upper levels. This a laminated-timber lattice 'gridshell' structure sealed with translucent inflated cushions of a high-strength lightweight fluoropolymer known as ETFE. Here it clads a retail building, letting in daylight and glowing at night from the light within. The roof structure oversails the ends of the building, forming deep curving cowls.

What has been built here is a place to go to for itself, not just to travel to and from. The new station emerges from a four-level over-site retail development including public rooftop sheltered gardens. This is a £500m project all made at once, with Canary Wharf Group contributing £150m of that. Given the huge increase in public transport connectivity, capacity and speed represented by the new railway to the growing development of Canary Wharf, its importance to the economy of London and the wider UK is great. You'll also notice how it opens up to the wider city. You can walk across bridges from here to the older communities of Poplar to the north, once redevelopment of the far side of North Dock is complete.

Or you can go up to the rooftop gardens, free to visit for everyone. Just as the building itself recalls the ships that used

| Crossrail Place development

| Stairs into Canary Wharf

| Roof garden at Crossrail Place

to use the West India Docks here from 1802, so the planting in the garden reflects the places around the world, east and west, where the ships went. There are restaurants at either end of the gardens. This was the first of the new station developments to be both started and finished and – given its prominent position in the water on the northern edge of Canary Wharf – one of the most immediately visible. The wider development, with its shops, restaurants and a cinema, was

opened in May 2015, more than three years before the gates across the ticket hall entrances were due to slide back to allow the first passengers in.

The wider urban realm, making this part of the Canary Wharf family of buildings and open spaces, is an integral part of the project. On the south side the technical requirement for flood absorption is met by a water garden running much of the

| Ceiling at Canary Wharf

© Nigel Young / Foster + Partners

| Water garden at Crossrail Place

| Crossrail Place; Ticket hall

| Ceiling detail at Canary Wharf

length of the building, where the water level rises and falls to regulate the dock. If you leave the station's western end and walk south, you cross the new Adams Place, landscaped with mirror pools beneath a high-level pedestrian access bridge, flanked by a sequence of raised planting beds. From here you can proceed, via steps or a lift, in a straight line to the Jubilee line station and Docklands Light Railway. Taken together, this makes the place a surface interchange station, requiring a stroll. But most people here will arrive and leave by one or other of the three rail options without needing to change between them.

And finally, this is a station where the necessary business of ventilation and pressure-relief shafts is expressed as part of the visible architecture. Expanses of clear water at either end mean no obstructions, so the vent grilles, treated as angled nozzles, project horizontally rather than rising in vertical shafts as is more common. Engineering and architecture thus become part of a fully integrated design, the workings of the railway system interleaving with the oversite retail development, and that very long roof remains uninterrupted. But you don't need to know all that. You'll probably just think it's a nice place to have lunch.

IN DETAIL
Glulam and ETFE roof
at Canary Wharf

The canopy roof of the retail and leisure development above the station is made from a lightweight, low maintenance and long lasting material called Ethylene Tetrafluoroethylene (ETFE) that allows the light to filter into the development over the station.

Custom House

FACTS & FIGURES

Station structure | **Above ground**

Passenger platform length | **202 metres**

Expected passenger numbers on the
Elizabeth line (daily) | **25,000**

No. of trains per hour
(peak, each way) | **12**

Architect's model of
Custom House proposal

To demonstrate their 'kit of parts' approach to this
surface station in the Royal Docks, the architects
first presented Custom House station in model
form, in pieces, in a mocked-up Hornby train set
box. They then opened the box and built it. This
was a nice bit of stagecraft but it also made sense.
Scaled up to real-life size, this was pretty much
how the whole thing was built – minus the Hornby
box. It is a fine piece of what's known as "offsite
construction". It is also, in its way, a classical
temple.

The site available to build it was very tight indeed, a strip
of old railway land between the existing Docklands Light
Railway and Victoria Dock Road with a line of power cables
passing overhead. Nearby is the northern landfall of the
"Emirates Air Line" cable car from Greenwich Peninsula across
the river. With little space for a conventional building site, it
made sense to deliver the building's various parts just when
they were needed for the construction process. Made in a
high-tech precast concrete factory in Nottinghamshire, the
main column-and-beam parts were packed onto low-loader
trucks for the 150-mile journey south.

DESIGN & BUILD

Architect | **Allies and Morrison**

Engineer | **Atkins**

Main contractor | **Laing O'Rourke**

Urban realm designs | **Ramboll**

BREEAM Rating | **Very Good**

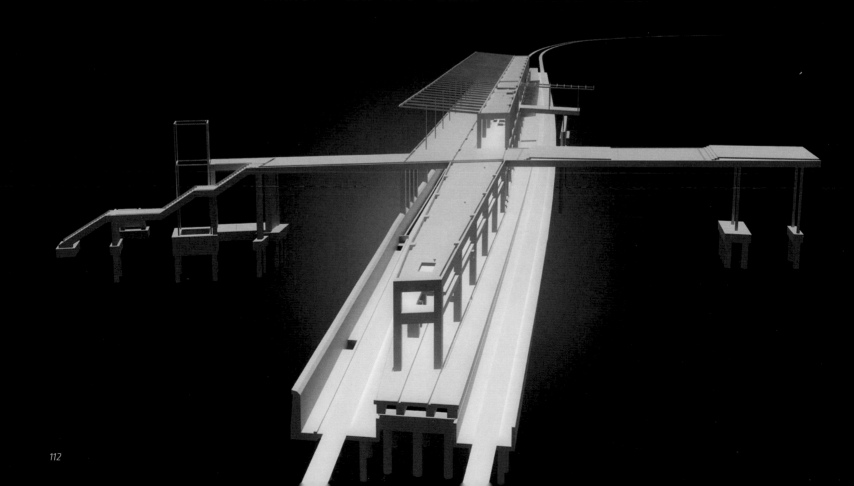

Architect drawing of the station from
the Victoria Dock Road

Space constraints also meant that the concourse had to be built over the tracks. This has the advantage of giving the station a two-storey presence, narrowing at the ends for stairs and lifts. It acts as an intermediate object between a giant-scale world – the vast shed of the ExCeL exhibition centre on the Royal Docks waterside immediately to the south, which will now be very well connected indeed – and the apartment and industrial blocks and 1960s terraces of Newham immediately to the north. The solidity of the smooth, pale concrete frame is offset by the more delicate canopy above the concourse, a steel-framed grid containing semi-transparent pneumatic 'pillows' of durable ETFE film. It's much the same stuff that you find on the biome domes of the Eden Project in Cornwall, has excellent light transmission, and is a fraction of the weight of glass. Beneath the concourse is an island platform with a subsidiary canopy on the southern side.

Architect drawing of the station
entrance at concourse level

| Custom House from Victoria Dock Road

It is a necessarily long building, in a very linear context, that is then given a literal twist. It could have been built as a straightforward orthogonal box. Instead, the architects picked up on the 18-degree angle between Victoria Dock Road and Freemasons Road which joins here. The entire building, right down to the paving details and the slightly rhomboidal shape of the columns and beams, is set out on this slight skew. It's as if the streets themselves had geologically extruded the building. And it is quite possible that most passengers won't even notice this. But what this device does is give the building a sense of energy and movement, something expressed in the underside of concourse level where the ceiling is given a folded-plate design of vaulting.

Being above-ground means that there is no need for the sizeable air-handling boxes common to the subterranean stations, and the openness and elevation provide good views. There are still several technical-equipment enclosures. These bring dashes of colour – predominantly yellow- to the composition, being clad in a mix of back-painted glass and patterned coloured metal.

As is part of the programme for nearly all the new stations, there is an urban realm improvement programme around Custom House. There's a new landscaped area with planting, wayfinding and much-improved lighting, along with cycle parking. This integrated scheme, being developed with the local council plans for the area, emphasises the way the station acts as a civic link across what is a transport barrier between the local community and the new commerce of the dockside.

| Ticket hall roof detail

Woolwich

FACTS & FIGURES

Station structure | **Box**

Passenger platform length | **241 metres**

Depth below ground | **14 metres**

Expected passenger numbers on the Elizabeth line (daily) | **56,000**

No. of trains per hour (peak, each way) | **12**

The Crossrail project's arrival in Woolwich, an area with a unique and colourful history, is the catalyst for intense regeneration; this will likely be one of the areas to benefit most from the new Elizabeth line service and associated developments.

This was the former home of the Royal Arsenal after which Arsenal football club was named, before they moved north to Highbury. Up on the hill above Woolwich you still have the impressive range of barracks worthy of St. Petersburg, while down by the river you find many surviving parts of London's military history dating back to the 17th century.

Here they made guns and explosives, with a foundry for everything from cannon-making to medals. Munitions were tested here, there was a military college and civilian products also made, such as industrial knitting frames and steam locomotives. It was a walled-off private world until it all finally closed down in the mid 1990s. Now it is an 88-acre housing redevelopment, with new blocks inserted among the restored historic buildings, the Thames Path passing by, and a new Elizabeth line station to serve it and the rest of the town, the former 'civilian' side where there is a rail and Docklands Light Railway interchange.

BIM model of Woolwich station

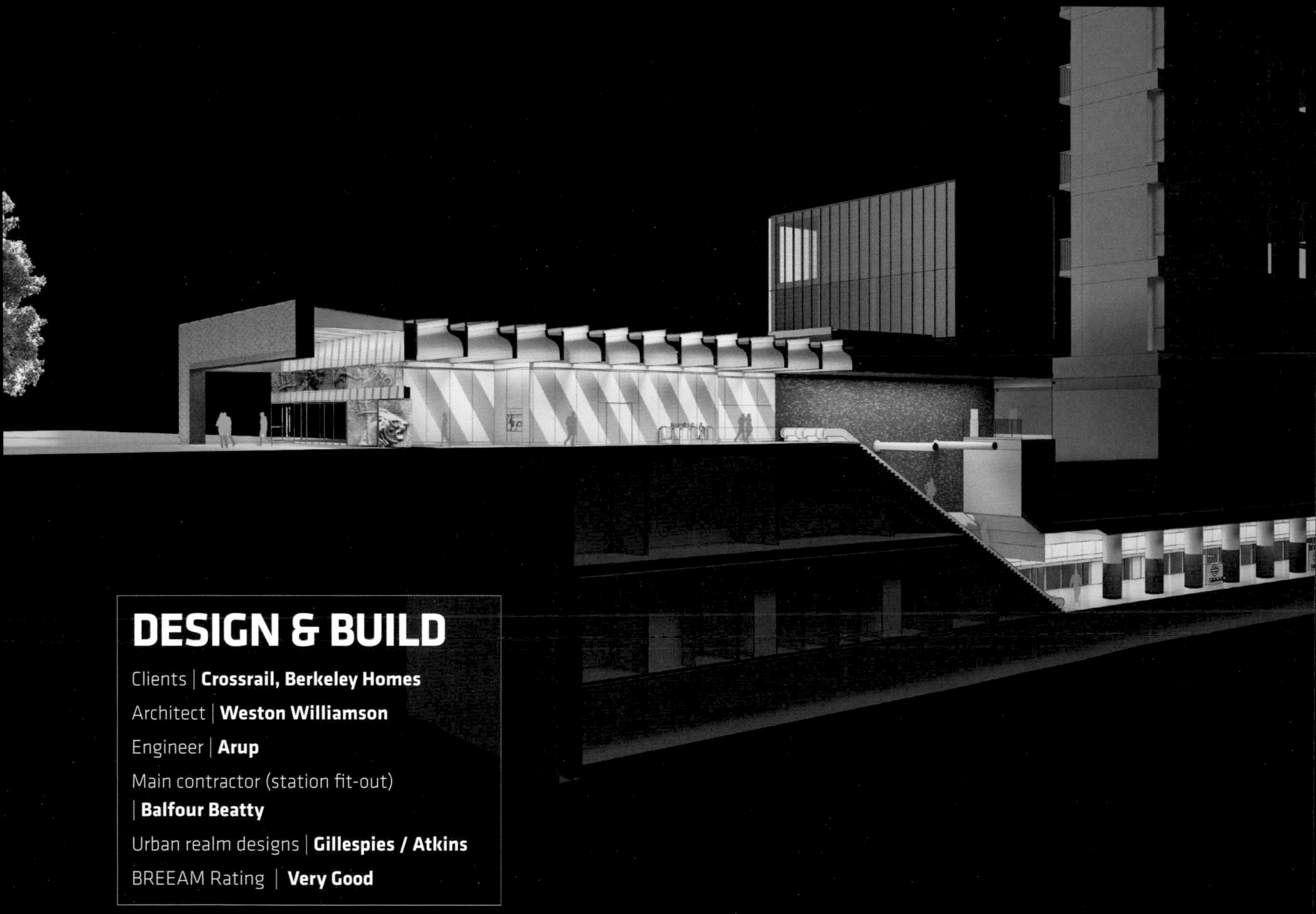

DESIGN & BUILD

Clients | **Crossrail, Berkeley Homes**

Architect | **Weston Williamson**

Engineer | **Arup**

Main contractor (station fit-out) | **Balfour Beatty**

Urban realm designs | **Gillespies / Atkins**

BREEAM Rating | **Very Good**

It's natural that the architects chose to pick up on this rich history when designing the station, which is of the 'box' variety with an island platform and a single entrance at the western end of the box close to the town centre. The box is sunk to the depth it needs for the route to dive beneath the Thames here, in a tunnel running across the river to North Woolwich. The Woolwich station box is designed to act as a base for a series of apartment towers above it with gardens above a podium of shops and cafes. This development is called Cannon Square, part of the Royal Arsenal Riverside development built by Berkeley Homes, who part-funded the new station. Another development at the eastern end of the station will provide 400 more much-needed homes for this newly connected region. Further east, the line emerges from the tunnel at Plumstead en route for its south-eastern terminus at Abbey Wood. But here, it's all about the Arsenal.

The station entrance is conceived as a simple, very broad concrete-framed portal spanning 20 metres within a long arcade beneath the apartment building above. The portal leads you into a ticket hall daylit via full-width glazing between the angled, acoustically-absorbent beams. Externally, the portal is clad in subtly-patterned brass – the asymmetrical patterning derived from that of the internal rifling of gun barrels, known as the Woolwich system and

| Ticket hall looking onto Dial Arch Square

| Ticket hall

| Woolwich, platform level

| Dead Man's Penny

| Dead Man's Penny imagery on station cladding

made here from the 1800s. The memory is inspired by the 1717 Royal Brass Foundry which stands nearby. From the entrance, the void housing the escalators is lined in the same brick as the ticket hall. These take you down to platform level, where the station box is up to 30 metres wide. It is a lofty space, with a marching row of fat columns down the centre carrying the buildings above.

The work of the foundry also inspires the surface treatment of the other cladding materials to the ventilation and emergency access shaft at the eastern end of the box. Bronze memorial plaques commemorating deaths caused by the First World War were also cast here in huge numbers, to be presented along with a memorial scroll to the soldiers' and civilian victims' families after the war. Four and a half inches in diameter, they were like very large coins, featuring Britannia, a lion, and the name of the person on each. Elements of these medals at giant scale are depicted in the perforations of the metal cladding, a further commemoration a century later.

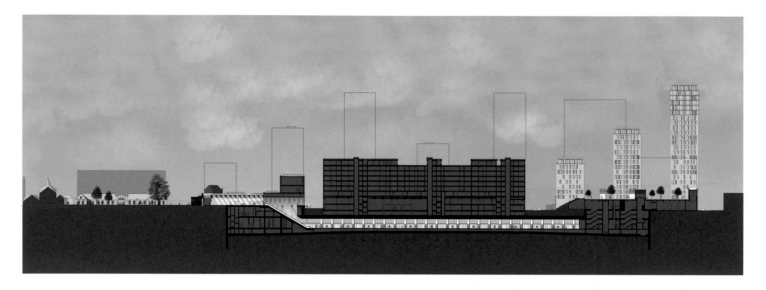

The station entrance portal also serves to frame the view out to the mature landscape of Dial Arch Square with trees beyond the pedestrian plaza. The station forecourt runs right along the eastern side of the square, which receives a paved threshold with seating, lighting columns and signage. From here new paths strike out across the square. Everything is step-free. On the south side, although high-density housing is built over the station here, the Royal Arsenal district as a whole contains a remarkable amount of landscaped open space, new and old. This stretches north to the river, and south across Plumstead Road via the recently-restored Royal Arsenal Gatehouse into Beresford Square with its market and live events. The urban realm design here ties everything together for the first time.

If the arrival of the DLR via a new tunnel was significant for Woolwich in 2009, the arrival of the Elizabeth line and its associated development will be a game-changer for what had, with the decline of its traditional industries, become one of the more deprived outer London districts. Now it is one of the most promising.

| Woolwich station proposed entrance

Abbey Wood

FACTS & FIGURES

Station structure | **Above ground**

Passenger platform length | **260 metres**

Expected passenger numbers on the
Elizabeth line (daily) | **52,000**

No. of trains per hour
(peak, both ways) | **12**

At Abbey Wood, terminus of the south-eastern branch of the Elizabeth line, the task was a much greater one than simply to expand an existing station. Here, uniquely on the line, the new building and its radically reworked surrounding urban realm act as a much-needed civic focus for a suburban area that had evolved in fits and starts from the 19th century without one. The Crossrail project will be more transformational here than anywhere else.

Occupying marshland first drained by monks and then used by the Royal Arsenal based in nearby Woolwich, Abbey Wood was still rural when the great designer-maker-poet William Morris built his Arts and Crafts "Red House", designed with Philip Webb, nearby. This was his country retreat: he would take the train from London and walk to the Red House from the station. It is still there, now owned by the National Trust. But the area steadily became built up with large housing estates. First came streets of houses built by local landowner the Cooperative Society. This was followed by a late 1950s "overspill estate" to house Eastenders displaced by slum clearance. All this was brutally wrenched apart in the mid

| *Abbey Wood station and forecourt*

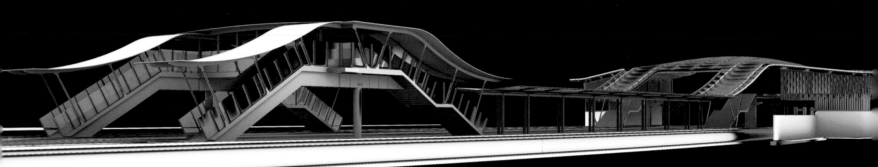

DESIGN & BUILD

Architect | **Fereday Pollard**

Urban realm design | **Urban Movement**

Engineer | **Tony Gee and Partners, WSP - Parsons Brinckerhoff**

BREEAM Rating | **Very Good**

Platform level, Abbey Wood

1960s when the new council-housing enclave of Thamesmead was built to the north. The planners drove a broad flyover through the centre of Abbey Wood to connect to this ambitious but flawed new mini-town, leaving the station as a sorry collection of ramps and underpasses in the middle of an urban mess. As Gertrude Stein said of her native Oakland, California, "There is no there there."

Now the area is scheduled to receive thousands more new homes, and it is time not only to connect the enlarged population to London and beyond, but also to heal the scars

of past planning mistakes. The local residents particularly wanted a proper station, something agreed by the boroughs of Greenwich and Bexley which come together here. The architects and landscape architects, along with Network Rail and the two boroughs, evolved a building and complementary urban realm that works hard to make a place where previously there was none.

Key to this is to tame the elevated highway, making it usable by pedestrians and cyclists. The station building is then set back. It is built over the railway tracks where the two new

| Platform level, Abbey Wood

lines come in and terminate while the existing Southeastern lines continue on through. This allows for a proper, granite-paved pedestrian concourse. From here the station building is shaped both to swoop down to platform level below, but also to link radically transformed civic spaces to either side at ground level. The integration of the new building with its surroundings through reformed public space will be to the benefit of residents and passengers alike.

From above the station is shaped rather like a manta ray, its zinc-surfaced 'wings' extending into canopies sheltering impressively-scaled staircases either side. Lifts emerge as architectural features flanking the station forecourt. The building with its ticket hall and shops makes great use of wood: framed inside with laminated larch beams, and clad on its flanks with a sustainable and durable African hardwood, above a warm brick base.

Glazed canopies run back along the platforms, with an escalator-equipped overbridge halfway down to allow easy changing between trains. Abbey Wood station gives the place an identity.

Finally there is a there there.

| *Urban realm and access, Abbey Wood*

Looking west

In west London, once the new route emerges into the open west of Paddington, an entirely different set of conditions apply. Here the task is to take existing stations – some of them in poor condition– and upgrade them so many more of us can use them. Improving the surrounding urban realm - a project initiated by Crossrail and now led by the London boroughs - is critical not just to make things pleasanter for us, not only to handle all the extra passengers, but also to help link what are often edge-of town stations with their centres. From east to west these are Acton Main Line, Ealing Broadway, West Ealing, Hanwell, Southall, Hayes & Harlington and (beyond the spur branching south to Heathrow) West Drayton. Beyond the Greater London boundary, the route moves on to Iver, Langley, Slough, Burnham, Taplow, Maidenhead, Twyford and Reading. The route is shared with the Great Western mainline railway, linking to the Underground at Ealing Broadway.

The busiest new station of this West London set is Ealing Broadway. Despite being in a very busy part of town, acting as an interchange between the various lines, the existing station is almost invisible, tucked beneath the concrete podium of a 1960s office development and hemmed in by roads, car parking and bin stores. The transformation here is as much to do with making a spacious and dignified station forecourt as it is with the covered station concourse. It is also to do with making a civic statement appropriate for the place once called "the Queen of the Suburbs". The complexities of land ownership here meant that three separate planning permissions for different parts of it were needed.

Now you will be able to approach and use the station much more easily. Bus shelters will be incorporated into the design of the area outside the station, led by the London Borough of Ealing. For pedestrians and cyclists, seating and bike parking will be provided. It will be easy to get across the road to the green oasis of Haven Green. The paved forecourt flows under a landmark timber-lined canopy with a delicate aluminium edge. Perched on slender steel columns, wrapping round the existing buildings with shops on each side, the canopy is picked out in blue light at night. Finally the railway has an appropriate gateway to and from the borough, signalling the arrival of the Elizabeth line.

Ealing Broadway station
Architects: Bennetts Associates

Hayes and Harlington station
Architects: Bennetts Associates

West Drayton station
Architects: Bennetts Associates

A glazed section of the canopy indicates the new wider entrance, leading you straight through into a larger, brighter, rectangular ticket hall, thence down to the platforms. It is clever design, this, making something with real urban presence out of what was previously little more than a rabbit-hole by the side of the road. Happening a little later than the central London stations, the rebuilding work has to be carried out while the station stays in use.

Elsewhere on this stretch, the main station upgrades typically involve repositioning the station entrance in a new building, with an improved landscaped pedestrian forecourt with added bike parking. Each station will have lifts providing step free access to the platforms. In many cases, these new structures will replace buildings which are hard to find, tricky to access, with zero scope for expansion.

Each one is different, but shares a common design approach of elegant glazed pavilions incorporating lifts to provide step-free access through the various changes of level. Hayes and Harlington is a key example: it looks straightforward enough but its apparent simplicity masks the way it brings together two streets on different levels, letting you move upwards into the covered concourse, and then down to the platforms – lengthened for the longer new trains. There's a lot of new development here, which prompted proposals for an ambitiously landscaped new triangular piazza, flanked with new apartments. Planted with trees, allowing for new bike

lanes and bike parking, providing step-free access throughout, all this is able to provide a massively improved setting for the station and a considerable uplift to the whole area.

At West Drayton, it's even more about the surroundings rather than the building. The broad Grand Union Canal passes right past it, but previously you'd never know. Set at the end of a cul-de-sac, it had no pleasant or direct way to walk to the centre of town, while the old station building was listed but run down. In the upgrade project the listed building is kept, restored and extended sideways in the same glass-pavilion manner as the other stations. The old and new parts form a single, larger station concourse, visually linked by a new canopy running along the front of both. A new pedestrian forecourt (previously car parking) is planned to lead straight to a pocket park with paths along the nearby Grand Union Canal.

From there, the plan may include a new pedestrian bridge that takes you across the canal to Yiewsley town centre, avoiding busy traffic junctions. Again seating, cycle parking, better bus stops and step-free access will be provided. Small though West Drayton is as a station, the wider effect of the Crossrail project here is proportionately large.

Looking east

In east London, the route continues on existing infrastructure to its terminus at Shenfield. As on the west, the urban realm around stations is designed to increase the permeability of the town centres.

All stations are changing in some way, to improve the experience of existing buildings and prepare for the arrival of the Elizabeth line. Ilford's station building will be wholly new, for which designs are progressing through the planning process. Significant refurbishments will upgrade Romford and Harold Wood and the remaining stations see a variety of improvements ranging from upgraded ticket halls and extended platforms to improved lighting, signage and furniture.

These works are complemented by Transport for London adding lifts and footbridges amongst other improvements, to ensure the whole route is accessible – and Network Rail's work to stations and tracks to modernise and underpin improving reliability.

Ilford represents a key transport interchange for the area, served by an incredible number of bus routes, comparable to that on Oxford Street. A new station is being designed to replace the current dated building, in conjunction with a substantial urban realm scheme that will allow the station to fulfil its potential as a key transport hub.

The proposed design outlines a bright, spacious, modern building in keeping with the glazed pavilions on the west of the route. Glazed frontages will deliver a wash of natural light into a much larger ticket hall designed to manage the growing numbers of passengers. The glazing is topped by a white seam metal roof and shouldered by coated, metal cladding designed to repel graffiti and reduce maintenance. Wider gatelines and new lifts to four platforms will improve accessibility and reduce congestion at the station. Transport for London is adding to these works by refurbishing the secondary entrance at York Mews to the west, improving legibility, pedestrian connections and street furniture.

| *Proposed urban realm at Romford*

| Proposed urban realm at Harold Wood

Outside on Cranbrook Road, widened footways, a realigned crossing and efficient placement of bus stops will ease the new station into its wider context and revitalise the townscape. The improved entrance on York Mews will benefit from a paved forecourt, enhanced by new trees. Better lighting, cycle parking and signage in these areas are all part of London Borough of Redbridge's ambitious plan to deliver a strong sense of arrival.

At Romford, an expansion and refurbishment of its ticket hall in conjunction with an expansive urban realm scheme will dramatically improve pedestrian space from the station toward the high street. Proposals being carried forward by London Borough of Havering will see the adjacent road, currently used for parking and delivery traffic, turned into a proper pedestrian space. This area will become the gateway to the new ticket hall which will be designed to be in keeping with the principles of spacious, bright and modern buildings across the route. Three new lifts inside the station will allow step-free access to the new, extended platforms; outside, enhanced landscaping, lighting and street furniture will ensure a high-quality step free experience beyond.

Harold Wood's ticket hall is being refurbished to transform the existing building into a welcoming, easy to navigate space. Three new lifts are being installed by Transport for London along with new customer information points and improved lighting to make the space brighter and appear larger. Crossrail has already installed a new footbridge which will be accessed from a rationalized car park and improved, pedestrianised station forecourt. This new forecourt will remove the dangerous conflict between pedestrians and motor vehicles; improve access for passengers with restricted mobility; create a stronger connection between the station and Harold Wood town centre; and provide a welcoming, focal point for passengers arriving at the station.

The new trains

Design consultants Barber Osgerby with TFL and Bombardier Transportation

The trains for the Elizabeth line, British designed and built, are a new, lightweight design by the makers which are then configured to be unique to London inside and out. Their special design includes not only the overall configuration of the trains but also the branding, which is London right down to the patterned, textured moquette seat coverings.

These nine-car trains are walk-through, so each forms a continuous interior more than 200 metres long. There's room in the stations for them to be even longer in future. Each will have a capacity of 1,500 people which is nearly twice as many as a Tube train. Being mainline trains running through the capital from Reading and Heathrow in the west to Shenfield and Abbey Wood in the east, they have much more space inside and are much faster than Tube trains also. A representative journey time from Shenfield in Essex direct to Bond Street in central London is 48 minutes. From Canary Wharf right across town to Heathrow Airport is 39 minutes. The aerodynamic cabs to the trains, another unique feature, are designed with the central tunnelled section in mind.

These are urban metro trains rather than long-distance inter-city trains, designed to transport the maximum numbers of people efficiently in and out of the capital. Air-conditioned, with Wifi and 4G connectability, they, like the stations will all be fully accessible. Key to fast journey times is for people to be able to get on and off quickly, so each carriage has three full sets of double doors each side. Doors are of the space-saving rattle-free 'plug' type which clamp inwards to shut. Clear space inside the doors also aids alighting and disembarking.

The lighter weight of these trains (made of steel-reinforced aluminium) means quicker acceleration times and reduced wear and tear. Other features include a responsive climate control and lighting system that adjusts itself constantly to keep people comfortable and save energy. Regenerative braking means that the trains generate electricity when slowing down, to put back into the system. All together this translates into 30 per cent less power use compared with conventional trains of equivalent type. They are designed to be ultra-reliable in operation, something partly achieved by electronic self-diagnosis for pre-emptive maintenance.

| Elizabeth line train interior

| Elizabeth line train interior

The new trains will have four dedicated wheelchair spaces per train

External livery is in blue and dark grey with flashes of the Elizabeth line purple, and light doors for contrast. For the train interiors, the designers went back into history to analyse what is considered to be one of the most aesthetically successful of all Tube train designs, the 1938 stock best known on the Bakerloo line which stayed in service for some 50 years. Next they considered the 'colour temperature' of the stations the trains stop at, so as to make sure they work seamlessly together – as if the platform extended into the train.

Inspired by these, the train interiors are designed to stay smart, with dark floor, light ceilings and walls, and huge windows. Grab handles are dark grey – bright colours not being needed against the light background. The moquette

seat fabric, from a Yorkshire company, is bespoke in a classic Transport for London seven-colour block pattern. There are three configurations of seating – longitudinal fixed, longitudinal tip-up, and cross-seats, plus four dedicated wheelchair spaces per train.

Key to the design is that the interiors should be able to "wear in rather than wear out". Durable materials are used that can take the heavy use demanded of these trains. After all, with ongoing maintenance they are designed to last for some 40 years.

Keeping with the idea that the interiors of the trains and stations at platform level should work as one – electronic information displays in the trains will give real-time travel updates on the situation up ahead. For trainspotters, the 66 trains ordered, with an option for 18 more, are a one-off type designated class 345. Finally, nobody likes a train that goes wrong, so TfL has demanded excellent reliability from the makers. While being low-cost to keep running, the trains are also designed with diagnostic equipment so they can sense when a part needs replacing. It's not something you can see, but it helps to ensure a smooth service.

TfL uses colour in a very purposeful way to assist customers with way finding and navigation – any new colours introduced have to be very carefully considered. The Elizabeth line purple was selected as being distinctly different to the red of the Underground and the individual colours as well as the Orange of the London Overground ensuring the service is clearly identified by customers. It was a happy coincidence that the colour is also associated with the Royal family.

The Elizabeth line is a new addition to the Transport for London family; a brother or sister to London Underground or London Buses. It retains the familial appearance of its siblings with TfL blue at its centre and a bold purple as its modal colour.

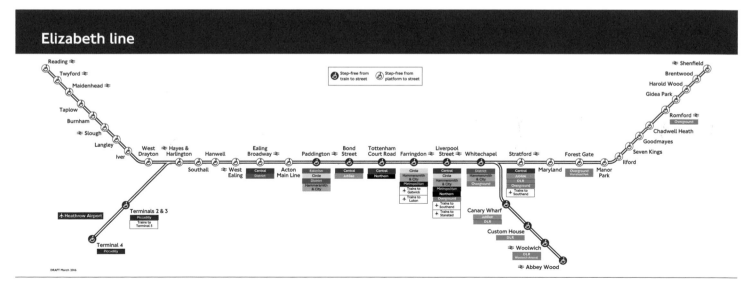

Elizabeth line

MAYOR OF LONDON

The culture line

Threaded through the Crossrail programme is an integrated public art programme. Although this was written into the Parliamentary Act authorising the line, it came with the proviso that the cost of it should be externally sponsored rather than coming from public funds.

The Crossrail Art Foundation, a charity, was set up to achieve this - a tall order given the dire economic situation at the time. Now the programme is bearing fruit, thanks in no small part to match-funding from the Corporation of London. Commissions to be made at a string of seven stations in the central area, from Paddington to Canary Wharf, will make this into a linear art gallery with the biggest viewing public imaginable. The potential audience is drawn from the estimated 200 million passenger journeys a year, plus all those who come into contact otherwise with the buildings and streetscapes of the line. London, after all, is partly defined by the healthy British contemporary art scene, not least the galleries here representing artists from around the world. So the decision was taken to partner with the best of those galleries – one per relevant station - in the search for the best artist in each case.

Good public art exists to enrich our everyday experiences. Its justification is our acceptance and appreciation of it, even in some cases our anger at it. It is best not 'safe'. It can baffle and intrigue as much as delight. Over time it should come to seem natural, part of what's being designed and built. Why were some 30 artists employed in a massive integrated art programme for New York's Rockefeller Center in the 1930s? Why does the original HQ of Transport for London, built in the 1920s, feature sculpture by the likes of Jacob Epstein and Henry Moore? You don't need to ask, today, though both were controversial in their time.

For Crossrail, contemporary artists were sought who had an international reputation and who could understand and respond to the scale and ambition of the project with a site-specific work. In each case a longlist of potential artists was put forward, to be whittled down to a shortlist of three by the curatorial panel. These three were then paid to develop proposals, and (usually) one was selected. The idea from the start was to integrate the art with the station architecture and engineering, giving as much freedom as possible to the artist. That way, each station became a canvas or narrative journey.

This is an evolving programme, with announcements yet to be made on some stations where artworks are developing and sponsorship being sought – for instance the White Cube Gallery is involved on proposals for the Bond Street western ticket hall on Davies Street. But here's a flavour.

Perhaps most prominent of those confirmed is at Paddington, by Brooklyn artist Spencer Finch, working with the Lisson Gallery and sponsored by Heathrow. His 'A Cloud Index' piece there is integrated into the laminated glass panels of the new station's canopy, sheltering the concourse below. It is 120 metres long by 18 metres wide, each panel being six metres by two metres. Finch's clouds (based on the main identifiable types) do what real clouds do – act as shading. Looking up through them to the real sky beyond will be special.

Tottenham Court Road will show the greatest concentration of artworks, with both the Crossrail project and London Underground contributing. Eduardo Paolozzi's colourful jazz mosaics in the Tube station are now restored (with sections that had to be removed in the expansion given to the University of Edinburgh for restoration and display). The new London Underground ticket halls and escalator shafts are walled with new geometric art pieces by French artist Daniel Buren. For Crossrail, here working with the Gagosian Gallery and sponsored by Almacantar and Derwent London, one key piece is a work by artist Richard Wright, applying a pattern in gold leaf to the ceiling of the Centre Point square escalator box. Making this could involve up to ten people at a time, lying on their backs

inches from the 10 metre by 20 metre pre-prepared concrete ceiling. It is the Sistine Chapel method of working.

At the western, Dean Street, end of the station you are getting into the night-time economy of Soho, which will be represented by a commission by artist Douglas Gordon accompanying you as you descend from street level. Digital artist, Michal Rovner with the PACE Gallery, is working on two platform-level pieces at Canary Wharf, sponsored by Canary Wharf Group, which are derived from people movement through the building.

Other works will appear in due course at the other stations in this central range – including both inside and outside the Broadgate ticket hall at Liverpool Street, where the Victoria Miro Gallery is involved. Works for Farringdon are being developed with Sadie Coles HQ. Other possibilities are being explored at Whitechapel. The programme is not rushed. It is about enriching the environments of the stations in a permanent way, thinking not just about the present but many decades, even more than a century, into the future.

There will be another permanent record of the Crossrail project, too: artist-in-residence Julie Leonard has worked since 2014 on a pictorial record of the places and people involved, working at speed making drawings and animations with a smartphone app. Together with recordings made in parallel, this will be a remarkable record of an extraordinary project.

Richard Wright, Detail of Turner Prize, 2009

The work was a handmade gold leaf piece, made directly onto the museum wall. It remained during the period of the exhibition and was removed at the end of the show.

Michal Rovner's initial proposal for Canary Wharf station

With grateful thanks to

Arup and Atkins in JV led the design for Tottenham Court Road, Custom House and Woolwich Crossrail stations. Each location presented different challenges from working out how to shoehorn the station around the Northern and Central lines at Tottenham Court Road, to designing a prefabricated station at Custom House to assist with construction on a constrained site. Separately from the JV Arup led the design for Canary Wharf Crossrail station and is working on Liverpool Street and Bond Street stations on behalf of the contractors. Atkins, in partnership with Grimshaw and GIA Equation, designed the architectural components that will create an integrated line-wide identity, and is working for the contractor at Farringdon station.

Joint venture BBMV consists of Balfour Beatty, BeMo Tunnelling, Morgan Sindall and VINCI Construction. The four leading international engineering companies worked together to deliver station and tunnel infrastructure at Liverpool Street and Whitechapel Stations for Crossrail.
Together the four businesses employ more than 200,000 people and have a combined turnover exceeding £40 billion world-wide, £10 billion of which is achieved in the UK.

Bechtel is part of the integrated management team on Crossrail. Along with Systra and Halcrow (a CH2M company) Bechtel is employed as the Project Delivery Partner for the central 21km tunnel section and eight new stations from Paddington through Canary Wharf to the southeast and through Pudding Mill Lane to the north east. Bechtel is also the delivery partner for Network Rail and its extensive Crossrail programme to upgrade the existing rail network.
Since 1898, Bechtel have completed more than 25,000 extraordinary projects across 160 countries on all seven continents. They operate through four global businesses: Infrastructure; Nuclear, Security & Environmental; Oil, Gas & Chemicals; and Mining & Metals.

BFK is a joint venture of BAM, Ferrovial and Kier comprising three of the world's leading rail, tunnelling, and civil engineering companies. As recognised industry leaders in infrastructure projects, they have an established capability in the delivery of complex railway and tunnel projects.
BFK was awarded the C300/C410 and C435 projects including the construction of 6.4km twin tunnels Royal Oak Portal -Farringdon, Bond Street and Tottenham Court Road station caverns, ventilation shaft and crossover at Fisher Street, 5 cross passages, East and West Ticket Hall construction at Farringdon Station plus 1.4 km of platform tunnels, cross passages and MEP works.

Costain–Skanska Joint Venture is responsible for constructing the new Elizabeth Line Paddington station, one of seven new underground stations to be constructed in London as part of the Crossrail Project.The station will be a key interchange hub allowing access and interchange between the existing Network Rail (NR) Paddington mainline station and with the London Underground (LU) Bakerloo, District, City, and Hammersmith & City lines.
Costain is one of the UK's leading engineering solutions providers, with a unique focus on major customers who are meeting national needs. The company's tunnelling expertise builds on the Channel Tunnel, Jubilee Line and HS1. Skanska is one of the world's leading project development and construction groups. In the UK, the company has delivered iconic structures like the Gherkin as well as major infrastructure projects such as upgrading the M25 motorway.

Great Portland Estates plc 'GPE' are a FTSE 250 Central London property investment and development company owning over £3.7 billion of commercial real estate. The existing portfolio consists of some 67 properties totalling 3.6 million sq. ft. (330,000 sq. m). GPE is an active and innovative developer with a current pipeline comprising 24 projects with a total potential area of 2.6 million sq. ft. (240,000 sq. m). We aim to deliver superior returns to our shareholders by unlocking the often hidden potential in retail and office property in Central London.

Global engineering and management company Mott MacDonald provided detailed design of Liverpool Street Station and Paddington Integrated Project. This covered all aspects such as civil, structural, architectural, mechanical and electrical as well as construction planning, passenger and transport modelling, and rail safety assurance. It also worked on eight of the 24 design contracts including leading-edge tunnelling, station, signalling, power, ventilation and safety systems design, and specifications for rolling stock, materials and workmanship. One of the world's largest employee-owned companies, with 16,000 staff, Mott MacDonald delivers sustainable outcomes for clients in 150 countries. It works on projects in the transportation, buildings, power, oil and gas, water and wastewater, environment, education, health and international development sectors.

Systra was appointed by Crossrail as part of the Project Delivery Partner (PDP) team to manage delivery of the Crossrail Project with Bechtel and Halcrow (a CH2M company). The company provide expertise in Railway Systems, Operations, Civil and Tunnel Engineering for the 21km of tunnels and eight new stations.
The Systra Group operates globally, a subsidiary of RATP and SNCF, it has 4,700 staff worldwide, providing engineering services, consultancy and transport planning in over 150 countries. In the UK Systra has circa 200 engineers/consultants across seven offices in the UK and Ireland.

WSP | Parsons Brinckerhoff provides technical expertise and strategic advice in the property & buildings, transportation & infrastructure, environment, industry, resources and power & energy sectors. They have designed Bond Street Station with an integrated multi-disciplinary team of engineers, architects, town, traffic and construction planners, cost managers and environmentalists. The design integrates into the confined surroundings of Mayfair and two constrained ticket hall sites. The method and sequence of construction has been an integral part of the design process including the over-site developments where we are the structural engineer for Great Portland Estates at Hanover Square. They are also working at Tottenham Court Road, Paddington and Farringdon on behalf of contractors, and elsewhere providing specialist Engineering Safety Management support.

BOND STREET

R.475

DOUBLE CURVATURE | SINGLE CURVATURE